WESTCHESTER COUNTY IN THE AMERICAN REVOLUTION

Neutral Ground

Stephen Paul DeVillo

THE History PRESS

Published by The History Press
An imprint of Arcadia Publishing
Charleston, SC
www.historypress.com

First published 2025

Manufactured in the United States

ISBN 9781467170307

Library of Congress Control Number: 2025943275

Respectfully dedicated to the historians, historical societies and "friends of" organizations that are working to preserve the heritage of The Bronx and Westchester.

CONTENTS

Acknowledgements 7
A Note on Place Names and Spellings 9
Introduction 11

1. Cow Boys and Skinners 17
2. Life in the Neutral Ground 26
3. The Year of the Hangman 33
4. The Westchester Guides 42
5. The Bloody Summer of 1778 49
6. The Burning of Bedford 64
7. Spies 75
8. "Whom Can We Trust Now?" 88
9. Pine's Bridge 97
10. Evacuation Day 107

Appendix. Who Was the Headless Horseman? 119
Notes 123
Bibliography 133
Index 139
About the Author 144

ACKNOWLEDGEMENTS

No book is written in isolation, and I am grateful to the many people who have given me support, encouragement, information and insights. My special thanks to:

My mother, Patricia Edwards Clyne, for her encouragement and use of her historical files and Westchester County book collection, and Frank Clyne, whose shared enthusiasm for geology and minerology informed my understanding of terrain and how landforms came to be where they are.

Jane Williams, who has often accompanied me in search of history.

Jorge Santiago, for sharing his researches into Bronx history.

Pelham Town Historian Blake Bell, for his detailed research into the history and folklore of Pelham.

Jonathan Kruk, Hudson Valley storyteller, for his insightful and entertaining renditions of our regional history and folklore.

Constance Kehoe, president of Revolutionary Westchester 250, for bringing together historians, reenactors and people in a shared appreciation of our Revolutionary history.

Michael Grillo, who as His Excellency General Washington has been indefatigable in bringing history to life.

Cynthia Kauffman and Debra Palazzo of the White Plains Historical Society and the Daughters of Liberty's Legacy for their unstinting efforts in preserving and commemorating the history of the Revolutionary War in Westchester.

Eastchester Town Historian Richard Forliano, for his support and insights.

Michael Virgintino, for his research contributions.

David Osborne, manager of the St. Paul's Church National Historic Site, for his generous assistance with my research.

Howard and Lea Waldman, battlefield residents and fellow Bronx River Ramblers, for their enthusiasm and support.

Particular thanks go to the Bronx River Alliance for its sponsorship of the Bronx River Rambles walking tours and to the Westchester Chapter of the American Association of University Women, which has hosted me in giving historical talks that helped hone my research.

The East Bronx History Forum and the Kingsbridge Historical Society and their dedicated corps of Bronx historians: Thomas X. Casey, Tom Colt, Jorge Santiago, Nick Dembowski, Nicholas DiBrino, Peter Ostrander, Rich Vitacco and Toby Z. Liederman of the Hutchinson River Restoration Project.

A number of local organizations deserve gratitude for their dedicated efforts to preserve history: the Bronx County Historical Society, the Croton Historical Society, the Dobbs Ferry Historical Society, the Dyckman Farmhouse Museum, the Eastchester Historical Society, the Friends of the Miller House, the Friends of the Odell House Rochambeau Headquarters, the Friends of the Stephen Ward House, the National Society of Colonial Dames in the State of New York, the North Castle Historical Society, the Scarsdale Historical Society, the Westchester Historical Society, the White Plains Historical Society, the Van Cortlandt House Museum and the Yonkers Historical Society.

Additional thanks to the Green-Wood Cemetery for its annual commemoration of the Battle of Brooklyn and to the Trenton Downtown Association and the Old Barracks Museum for their annual sponsorship of the Patriots Week commemorations and reenactments of the Battles of Trenton.

A note of appreciation to Michael G. Kinsella, acquisitions editor, and Ryan Finn, senior editor, at The History Press for their work in bringing this book to press.

Lastly, a salute to the Brigade of the American Revolution and in particular to the men and women of the Second and Fifth New York Regiments, whose dedicated participation in numerous reenactment events in the New York area make history "real" in ways books alone cannot achieve.

A NOTE ON PLACE NAMES AND SPELLINGS

Westchester County in the 1770s included all of the present-day Bronx, which was annexed by New York City between 1874 and 1895 and established as a county in 1914. Local pride insists on capitalizing The Bronx, and so as a lifelong Bronxite I'll follow this fashion when referring to the current New York City borough.

The name of the Bronx River was often rendered "Brunks River" on period maps, but for clarity's sake I'll use the standard version, as I will with Spuyten Duyvil, despite a bewildering variety of spellings.

Dutchess County included present-day Putnam County, which wasn't split off until 1812. Throughout the book, I'll refer to Dutchess and Westchester Counties according to their eighteenth-century extents. Although named for Mary of Modena, Duchess of York, Dutchess County retains the archaic spelling with the *t*.

There were several spellings of the name of DeLancey, but I've chosen to adhere to this version.

"Cow Boy" was the usual spelling of the term in the 1700s, and I follow it for sake of period authenticity and to make it clear that the term as used here has nothing to do with Hopalong Cassidy. Likewise, I follow the old spelling of the Saw Mill River.

People in the eighteenth century had a curious way of expressing themselves that may appear amusingly eccentric to modern eyes, with variable spellings and capitalizations and an almost Shakespearian syntax. To preserve the flavor of the times, I've kept to the original forms of quotations.

INTRODUCTION

Amid the well-manicured yards and designer-built houses of the Westchester suburbs, or along the sidewalks of industrial Bronx neighborhoods, the commuter or passerby might not realize that he or she is crossing a battleground.

A park ranger once recalled a visitor who remarked, in all apparent innocence, that he found it curious that so many Civil War battles took place in national parks. Today's Westchester and The Bronx may lack a national park on the grand scale of a Saratoga or Gettysburg battlefield, but together they too were once a battlefield in what was in effect America's original civil war, the American Revolution.

There is history that people seek to remember, and then there is history that people, at least at first, may have preferred to forget. Many events that took place in the Neutral Ground between 1777 and 1783 belong to the latter category, when neighbor turned on neighbor in the name of King George or the Continental Congress—or out of mere envy, greed or spite. Those of us who may recall the well-tailored heroes of our schoolbook illustrations have since learned that the American Revolution was a murkier and messier business but nonetheless heroic for all that. It was also more socially diverse, an aspect that I strive to emphasize.

The Neutral Ground was understood to be all of Westchester County south of the Croton River, which then included the present-day Bronx, all the way down to the banks of the Harlem and East Rivers and Long Island Sound. Historic events seldom stop at man-made limits, so when relevant I refer to events outside of, or on the fringes of, Westchester County, such as Dutchess, Orange and Fairfield Counties, or happenings farther afield that had an impact on the situation in the Neutral Ground.

The story picks up where my previous book, *The Battle of White Plains*, left off. Although Westchester and The Bronx would see no more major battles after the autumn of 1776, the bitter small unit fighting in the Neutral Ground would play an important part in the Revolutionary conflict, including what was arguably the most crucial incident of the entire war, which took place on a dusty road linking Tarrytown and Sleepy Hollow.

In following the story of the Neutral Ground, I've integrated local legend and folklore into the narrative, albeit always labeling it as such. The reason is that this is as much a history of a place as it is of a sequence of events. Folklore is sometimes a way people have memorialized the past and often as not contains a kernel of fact covered by the fluff of fancy. At the very least, it provides an entertaining look at how hearsay has mangled history. I therefore include these local legends, albeit with a caution not to believe everything the old-timers tell you.

I also make references to existing buildings and monuments that stand as silent witnesses to the events described. These will help the readers orient themselves and point out that history here has not entirely vanished but may be physically accessed today.

The history of the Neutral Ground is colorful, complex and not always pretty, and that is the tale told here. Despite 250 years of urban and suburban development, traces of the Revolution in our area are all around us in the form of monuments, historical markers, museums and historic houses, and they are not hard to find. My hope is that this book will encourage readers to explore these traces of the past, engage with historical societies and reenactors and get to know our rich legacy of the American Revolution.

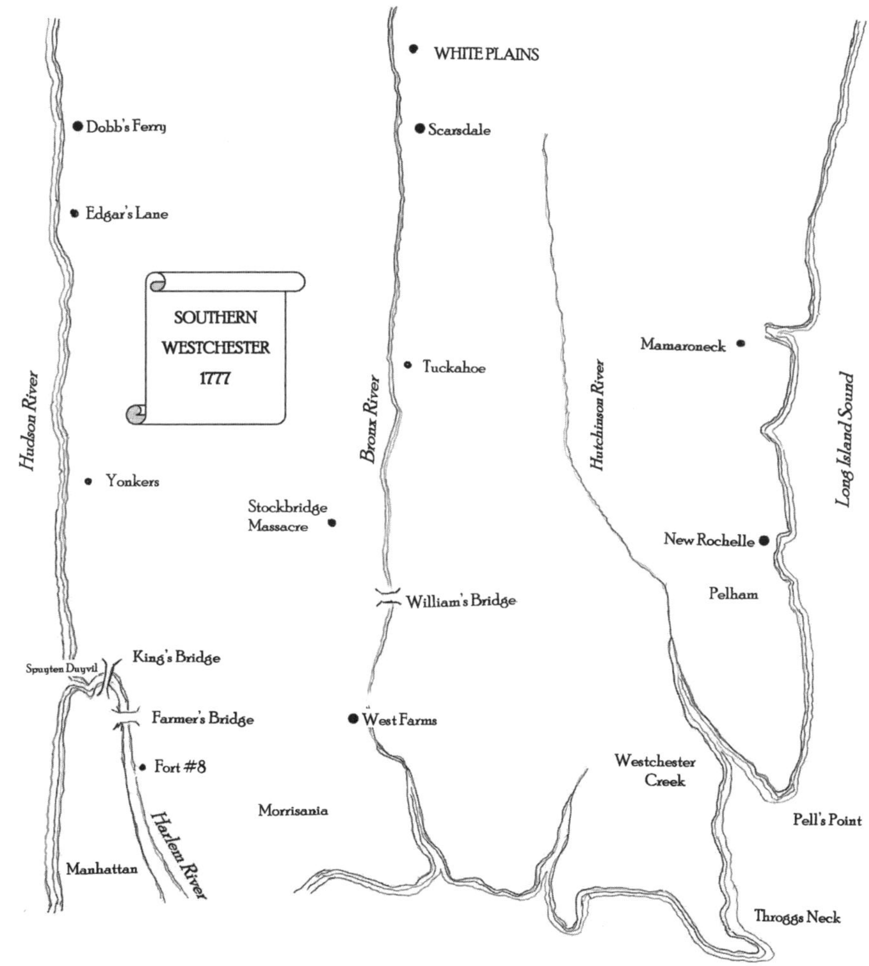

Southern Westchester. *Map by author.*

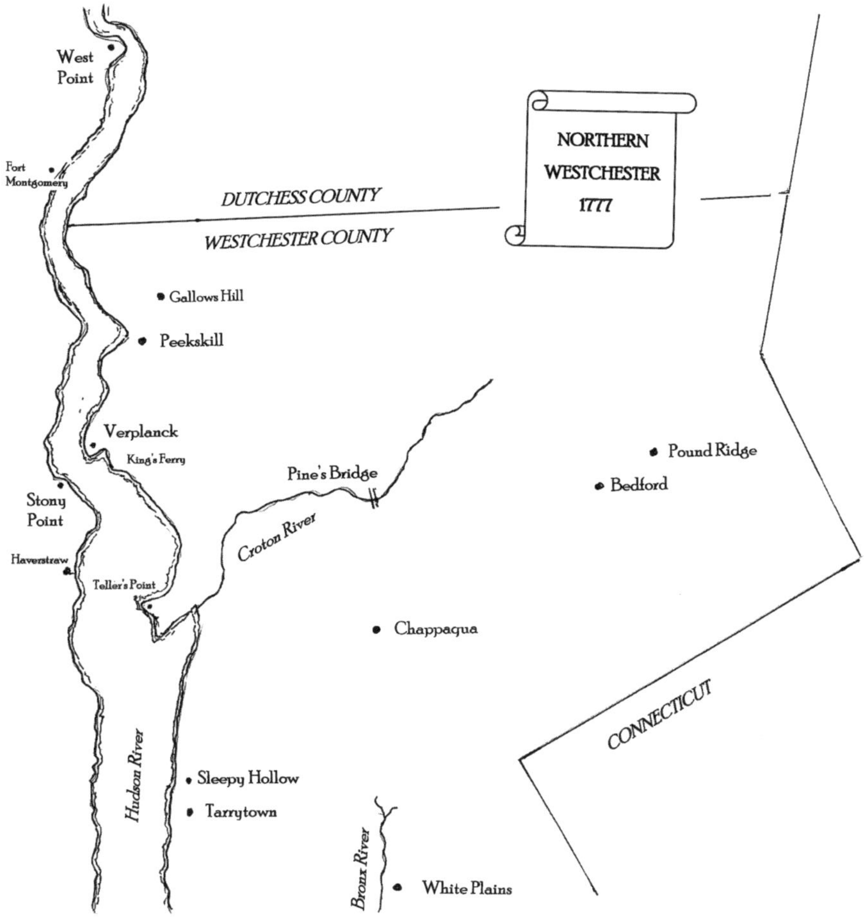

Northern Westchester. *Map by author.*

Chapter 1

COW BOYS AND SKINNERS

The Battle of White Plains on October 28, 1776, was a battle from which both sides retreated. Unable to bring Washington to bay or dislodge his forces from their hilly defenses, the British army quit the field on November 5, 1776, to march south to Manhattan Island and storm Fort Washington instead. Five days later, Washington took his tattered army north to the fastness of the Hudson Highlands.

The residents of central and southern Westchester may have breathed a sigh of relief seeing the armies depart, but their troubles were only beginning. For the rest of the war, Westchester County from the Croton River to Kingsbridge would be a no-man's-land known as the Neutral Ground.

Geology determined that south-central Westchester would not lend itself to occupation by either side. The region is characterized by two rocky ridges that run north–south, with the Bronx River in between and a flat glacial outwash plain running eastward down to Long Island Sound. South of the Croton and Byram Rivers, the Bronx, Saw Mill, Hutchinson and Mamaroneck Rivers flow generally north to south. All of this made it difficult to anchor an east–west defense line on naturally defendable terrain.

Sharp upthrusts of bedrock north of White Plains marked the beginning of the rugged Hudson Highlands, a natural stronghold for American forces seeking to interdict the upper Hudson River and guard the rich iron-producing areas in the Ramapo Mountains. A dozen miles to the south at the lower end of the county, high ground around the Harlem River and Spuyten Duyvil Creek shielded the Kingsbridge crossings to Manhattan.

There was little reason for either side to tie down valuable troops to hold the intervening terrain between White Plains and Kingsbridge.

As the focus of the war shifted to New Jersey at the end of 1776, with Washington's epic "retreat to victory" that ended on the Delaware River, it was clear that the British would not attempt to occupy south-central Westchester, leaving in the lurch the many Loyalists in the area.

The people of the nascent United States were far from united in favor of independence, and the people living in the Neutral Ground were deeply divided, with perhaps half or more being Loyalist or Loyalist-leaning. While some kept quiet, others were outspoken in their opinions. The Anglican minister Reverend Samuel Seabury Jr. was a prominent Loyalist in lower Westchester, leading his congregants in prayers for King George from his pulpits in St. Peter's Church in the town of Westchester[1] and St. Paul's in Eastchester. An imposing, barrel-chested man, Seabury commanded attention wherever he spoke and let nobody doubt where his commitments lay. Seabury rallied Loyalist opinion in the 1774–75 "Pamphlet War" that preceded the outbreak of fighting, advancing what to many were cogent arguments on behalf of the royalist government. Crossing swords (or rather quills) with a young Alexander Hamilton, Seabury maintained that the only sensible choice anyone could make amid the political contentions was to cling to the king. Swayed by his arguments, many did.

Seabury's pamphlets were issued anonymously in keeping with the style of the day. Seabury signed himself "A Westchester Farmer," but it was understood by Patriots and Loyalists alike that he was the author. This made him a target for Patriot retaliation, and he sought refuge in British-occupied New York City, where he would help guide General Howe's botched invasion of lower Westchester that led to the Battle of White Plains. The British pullback from White Plains left both St. Peter's and St. Paul's in unsecure territory, and with his name on the rebel hit list, Seabury returned to Manhattan, never to preach in Westchester again.[2]

While Samuel Seabury fought his war with a quill pen, others were moved to take up arms. Those who had openly come out and joined the king's forces had no choice but to abandon their homes and follow the army. More lukewarm Loyalists and those trying to maintain neutrality (such as the area's substantial Quaker population) opted to stay put, hoping that the lack of overt action on their part would keep them safe long enough for the rebels to lose the war. The war didn't quickly end, leaving those facing violence and property seizures to flee south to seek safe haven on the coattails of the British army. Such a safe haven would be provided by James DeLancey.

Patriot violence and intimidation drove many Loyalists from their homes, while others enlisted in the British service. *Library of Congress.*

DeLancey's estate occupied the approximate footprint of today's Bronx Zoo, in the West Farms neighborhood of The Bronx. West Farms was well situated to shelter Loyalists fleeing from the north. Situated at the southern end of the narrowing peninsula, to the west it was protected by the Harlem River and the string of British outposts guarding the approaches to Manhattan. To the east lay the deep waters of the Bronx River Estuary. On the south, the treacherous waters of Hell Gate and the boggy marshes lining the shore made hostile incursions from that direction unlikely.

Immediately south and west of the DeLancey estate were the lands of the Morris family (present-day Morrisania), home of Declaration of Independence signer Lewis Morris and his raffish half brother Gouverneur Morris.[3] These arch-rebels posed no worry to James DeLancey, as they were absent in Philadelphia, leaving their mother, Sarah Gouverneur Morris, herself an avowed Loyalist, in charge of the estate.

Intermarriage with the elite of colonial society divided the Morris family. While Lewis and Gouverneur Morris were early and enthusiastic adherents to the cause of independence, two of their sisters, Catherine and Isabella, were married to Loyalists, and brother Staats Long Morris was an officer in the British army. On the other hand, two of their merchant uncles supplied the Patriots with cannons shipped from their storehouse on Curaçao.[4]

The loyalism of Sarah and other members of the Morris family made little difference to the Loyalist refugees who occupied the estate, who revenged themselves on Lewis and Gouverneur by ransacking the Morris family vault and scattering the remains found therein. As late as 1911, human bones would be turned up in the vicinity.[5]

Like many families in Westchester, the DeLanceys were not unanimous in their attachment to the Crown. General Oliver DeLancey's cousin Alice DeLancey was married to Ralph Izard, a South Carolina delegate to the Continental Congress. James's younger brother, another Oliver, had been an officer in the Royal Navy who, refusing to fight against the Americans, resigned his commission at the outbreak of the war.[6] Warren DeLancey likewise joined the British army and distinguished himself at the Battle of White Plains but afterward resigned his commission. Warren's motives are unclear, but both he and Oliver remained in West Farms after the war.[7]

There was no question as to where James DeLancey's own loyalty lay. He was the son of the recently deceased Peter DeLancey, known as "Peter of the Mills," who owned a lucrative set of watermills at the southern end of the Bronx River Gorge that had been grinding grain and sawing lumber for more than a century. The DeLanceys were an old Huguenot merchant family with substantial landholdings in Manhattan and Westchester, and the Bronx River mills, combined with a small river port at the head of the estuary, lent Peter DeLancey's West Farms estate economic sustainability.

Although removed from the political power center of lower Manhattan, DeLancey's place was a popular destination for a visit to the country, and the well-connected DeLanceys had a high-ranking guest list. A highlight of such a visit was a leisurely carriage ride along the Bronx River, with a stop at the mysterious Rocking Stone, a ninety-ton glacial erratic balanced on a smooth bedrock outcropping that remains today as a landmark in the Bronx Zoo. The men would get out of the carriage and put their muscles into rocking the boulder back and forth while the women looked on in wonder.[8]

Many Westchester families were divided by the war. Alice DeLancey was married to Ralph Izard, a prominent member of the Continental Congress. *Library of Congress.*

Although the death of Peter made James the apparent heir of the West Farms estate, the property was actually held by his mother, Elizabeth DeLancey. Descended from one high-status colonial family (the Coldens) and married into another (the DeLanceys), Elizabeth Colden DeLancey was as close to aristocracy as you could find in colonial New York. Brooking no impertinence from anybody, she had gone as far as to name her new mansion overlooking the mills Union Hill in honor of the union of England and Scotland, leaving no doubt about her attachment to Great Britain and her firm belief that the colonies should remain likewise.[9]

James DeLancey was in an outstanding position to be a Loyalist leader in the growing civil war in Westchester. In colonial days, when provincial politics were based less on ideology but were instead divided between an in-crowd and an out-crowd, the DeLanceys remained close to the political establishment. James's grand-uncle (also named James) served as chief justice and later as lieutenant governor of New York.

Beneficiaries of the established social order, the DeLanceys had little sympathy for those who would challenge it. James's uncle Oliver served as an associate justice on the 1766 *Crown v. William Prendergast* case that tried William Prendergast for high treason for opposing the land seizures by the Philipse family in Dutchess County. (Prendergast was sentenced to death though later pardoned.) With the British invasion of New York in the summer of 1776, Oliver was appointed a brigadier general and raised a 1,500-strong DeLancey's Brigade of Loyalist volunteers. James himself had been the high sheriff of Westchester County before the war and thus had a good grasp of the county's geography as well as its political landscape.

In the wake of the British withdrawal from Westchester in the autumn of 1776, Patriot violence forced many Loyalists to seek refuge with DeLancey in West Farms. Building a hut village in the vicinity of today's St. Mary's Park to house the incoming refugees and a blockhouse to guard the bridge over the Bronx River, DeLancey set about organizing the able-bodied men into a militia force with which to strike back at the detested rebels.[10] Known variously as DeLancey's Refugees, the Westchester Refugees, the Associated Loyalists or, briefly, the Westchester Chasseurs, DeLancey's band was never part of the British military establishment, even though James's uncle Oliver could have provided him with a connection to the British high command. It isn't clear why the British never incorporated DeLancey's Refugees into their forces as they did with other Loyalist units; perhaps James, preferring to run his own private war along the Bronx River, was happy to leave it that way.

Hon. Col. James De Lancey.

At his West Farms estate on the Bronx River, James DeLancey organized Loyalist refugees to raid Patriot farms. *From W.A. Calnek's* History of the County of Annapolis *(1897).*

DeLancey's Refugees would soon acquire another name. Ensconced in their West Farms stronghold, the Refugees had a cash flow problem. Although the British army would occasionally summon them to report for paid temporary service, this would amount to only fifty-two days out of the entire war. To feed themselves and raise funds for other necessities, the Refugees would turn to cattle rustling, seizing cattle from Patriot farms and driving them to the British outposts at Kingsbridge. Subsisting on often rancid rations of salted pork and beef shipped in from across the Atlantic, British commissaries were eager for fresh beef on the hoof and were willing to pay for it in gold and silver.

Innumerable western movies have associated the word *cowboy* with the nineteenth-century Wild West, but the first cowboys in fact splashed across the eighteenth-century Bronx River. And the term definitely did not mean the good guys in the white hats. Originally a word meaning ne'er-do-well hangers-on, DeLancey's raiders were termed "Cow Boys" for their habit of stealing people's cattle. The term would remain an insult throughout the 1800s, and boys in Westchester would play "Cow Boys and Skinners" long before they switched to "Cowboys and Indians," with the Cow Boys as the bad guys.[11]

DeLancey's Refugees aside, the British command was reluctant to recognize or give support to ad hoc groups of Loyalist fighters. It may have been professional pride, believing that the Redcoats could end the rebellion without help from the locals, or perhaps they feared worsening a civil war by enlisting Americans to fight Americans. As they recognized the need for Loyalist assistance after 1776, they insisted on such units being part of a "Provincial Corps," organized under British military discipline and led by duly commissioned British officers.

Independent Loyalist units would eventually gain a semblance of legitimacy from the Honourable Board of Associated Loyalists, convened in British-occupied New York City in 1779, which openly encouraged Loyalist bands to plunder the property of those deemed to be rebels. While it could offer little in terms of financial or material support to such posses, the board could extend a gloss of official sanction to their depredations. Waterborne raiders could have their whaleboats or small craft officially commissioned as British warships to avoid the taint of piracy. Likewise, Loyalist leaders could get themselves commissioned as British officers, although it is doubtful whether any of this would spare a captured raider from a summary hanging.

DeLancey's horsemen had by that point been raiding Westchester for years, but some of his squad leaders gratefully accepted lieutenant's commissions, which would at least come in handy for their reimbursement applications after the war. James DeLancey himself was commissioned a colonel in the British army, but he nevertheless harbored no illusions as to his fate if captured. Aware of a price on his head, he would rarely lead his troops in the field, but instead organized and dispatched raids from the security of Morrisania.

The American counterpart of the Cow Boys were the Skinners. Unlike the Cow Boys, the term *Skinners* did not originate in any one particular organization, but rather was a generic term applied to raiders claiming allegiance to the independence side.

The term's origins are uncertain. It may have begun as a nickname for a Loyalist unit organized by Brigadier General Cortlandt Skinner. Its application to Patriot raiders may owe as much to its use in James Cooper's novel *The Spy* (and later on Washington Irving's *A Chronicle of Wolfert's Roost*) as it did to its use in the 1770s.[12]

The word may also have arisen from vengeance and vandalism. This author suspects that the name of Skinners may be a reference to the extreme destruction practiced by rebel raiders on the homes of Loyalists. Skinners were said to do more than rob the homesteads: they would take the time to trash the joint, notably going as far as to rip down the wallpaper—that is, "skin" the walls—as a parting disrespect to affluent Tory farmers. Another explanation is that the Skinners made a habit of robbing victims of their clothing.[13]

Throughout the county, there were various hideouts, safe houses and rallying points for one side or the other, such as "Rebel Hollow" along the Saw Mill River near Elmsford, with "Buttermilk Hill" a few miles to the west serving as a rendezvous for Cow Boy cattle rustlers. Local legend has it that a rock formation known as the "Bears' Den" in today's New York Botanical Garden was a gathering point for American partisans. This may have something to do with the fact that the forest along the Bronx River Gorge is one of the last remaining patches of never-timbered virgin woodland in New York. Although the firewood-hungry British sent woodcutting parties far and wide, they never cut these woods, perhaps for fear of American bushwackers.[14]

Whether Skinners or Cow Boys, the raiders bedeviling the Neutral Ground may have claimed allegiance to one side or another but, in fact, were more often opportunists who cared little for the opinions of those they plundered. Across the Hudson in Orange County, Claudius Smith gained fame as a counterpart to James DeLancey. Born in Brookhaven, Long Island, and a veteran of the French and Indian War, Smith proclaimed his allegiance to King George and recruited three of his sons as the nucleus of a gang that for more than two years would terrorize southeastern Orange County. Like James DeLancey, Claudius Smith earned the epithet of "Cow Boy," and again like DeLancey, he chose to pursue his own private war with little support from the British. Smith also copied DeLancey's business model by driving stolen cattle and horses down to Paulus Hook, where British purchasing agents would pay him in hard currency.

The depredations of Smith's Cow Boys resulted in a $1,200 bounty placed on his head, and he was eventually caught by American whaleboat raiders while hiding out with relatives in Smithtown, Long Island. Taken back across Long Island Sound and through Westchester County, Smith was handed over to the Orange County sheriff in Poughkeepsie. He was tried and hanged in Goshen on January 22, 1779, along with two of his sons.[15]

Claudius Smith's larcenous career gave rise to legends, one of which relates that his mother had once said that the wayward Claudius would die with his boots on, a byword for suffering a violent death. Standing on the scaffold, Claudius spotted his mother among the crowd of onlookers and kicked his boots off just to make his mom a liar. It is said that his skull was eventually exhumed and embedded in the lintel over the entrance to the 1840 courthouse that still stands in the town of Goshen. Another tale has it that he secreted a treasure in or around what is known as "Claudius Smith's Den" atop a mountain in present-day Harriman State Park.

There seems to be no corresponding legend of bandit treasure in the Neutral Ground. Perhaps, like the pirates of old, Westchester's Cow Boys and Skinners preferred to spend their ill-gotten gains rather than sock them away for another day, a day that they were not likely to see.

Chapter 2

LIFE IN THE NEUTRAL GROUND

For those who remained, the Neutral Ground was an edgy place, where neighbor suspiciously eyed neighbor, where old grudges and rural peeves could escalate into violence and where the dust of distant horsemen could mean approaching disaster.

Westchester's prosperous farms made the territory a resource for both sides, and the seizures and confiscations began early. Days after the British landing at Throggs Neck in October 1776, the Patriot government of New York State appointed a commission headed by Stephen Ward to purchase all beef cattle in lower Westchester and drive them to the army in northern Manhattan. Farmers were enjoined to get on with threshing their wheat crops to produce straw that could be sold to the army. The purchase price for cattle and straw was determined by the commissioners and usually paid in Continental currency, which depreciated while one looked at it. Washington in the meantime ordered officials to remove all cattle from the coastal areas of the county to deny them to the British, as well as to kill them if necessary.[16]

The autumn of 1776 would be only the beginning of a seven-year-long war that would leave central and southern Westchester devastated.

Although dubbed the "Neutral Ground," southern Westchester was a place where none was allowed to remain truly neutral. On the principle of "those who are not with us are against us," people insisting on their neutrality were often assumed to be on the enemy side and thus fair game for abuse or plunder. It was especially hard for members of Westchester's Society of Friends, commonly known as Quakers. The county was the longtime

Caught between two fires, Westchester's substantial population of pacifist Quakers sought to remain neutral in the conflict, although their neutrality was respected by neither side. *Library of Congress.*

home to a substantial Quaker population, who, unwelcome in Puritan New England, began settling in Westchester in the 1670s. By the 1770s, they were an established presence in Rye, Harrison, Scarsdale and Chappaqua, as well as areas of adjoining Dutchess County.[17]

As committed pacifists, the Quakers spurned militia service, payment of war taxes or even accepting Continental currency, and individuals enlisting for service on either side would be formally excommunicated, or "read out" from their local meeting. Few respected the Quakers' neutrality, however, and the pressures of the war opened rifts within their families. At his ridge-side home overlooking New Rochelle, James Pugsley struggled to maintain his Quaker principles, even though three of his sons were serving in Loyalist units, while his brother William wore a sword as a captain on the rebel side. James had also found himself an involuntary host to the British army when in October 1776 General Howe requisitioned his home as a temporary headquarters.

Howe eventually moved on, leaving Pugsley to be a target of rebel raiders. Convinced that the affluent Pugsley had a stash of cash hidden in the house, they came to seize it one day and, frustrated by Pugsley's denial, dragged his daughter Hannah out to the barn and proceeded to repeatedly hang her to the brink of unconsciousness to extort the location of the treasure. After several attempts, Hannah was on the point of death when a British cavalry patrol, alerted by one of the family's slaves, arrived in the nick of time. The enslaved servant, also named Hannah, cut Hannah down and succeeded in reviving her, and the Skinners fled with empty sacks. In belated gratitude, Hannah Pugsley emancipated the enslaved Hannah in 1799.

Sometimes convivial social skills could blunt the impact of a raid. According to Ferris family lore, when raiders arrived on the doorstep of Marianna "Myanna" Hunt near Throggs Neck, she invited them in for hotcakes and drinks. It was a cold winter afternoon, and the raiders happily found seats by the fireplace, where Myanna plied them with hot mulled cider. The fermented cider was fortified with a splash of rum, and the raiders gladly dawdled over their free drinks. By the time they got up to get on with the raid, Myanna's cattle had been secured by neighbors, who gathered around the farmstead with weapons in hand. The raiders wisely called it a day and headed back to wherever they had come from.[18]

As the war went on, life in the Neutral Ground became increasingly frightful, and many fled seeking safe refuge. Loyalists targeted by Patriot vigilantes made their way south to British lines, either to James DeLancey's Loyalist enclave in West Farms or to a number of refugee camps that sprang up around Manhattan island. Living in improvised shelters, life for these refugees was difficult at best, and to get by, many had to rely on scavenging, odd jobs or even prostitution. Adding to the misery, camps were often located in or near marshy ground, such as Lispenard Meadows on the lower west side of Manhattan, where malaria took its toll. Worse still was "Canvass Town," where amid the ruins of the Great Fire of 1776 destitute residents and refugees camped in cellar holes and flung scavenged sail cloths over charred beams to create some sort of shelter.

A fortunate few of the displaced had the resources with which to relocate. Brom Dyckman's family, for example, abandoned their northern Manhattan farm and were able to rent a farm in the safer locale of Cortlandt Manor.[19] For most farmers in the Neutral Ground, though, the family's wealth was tied up in their farms, and they faced a harsh choice between securing their lives and maintaining their livelihoods.

Some tried commuting, tending their wheat fields by day and fleeing to a safe haven at nightfall. Others sought to hide out in their fields. One man in today's Hartsdale left his house empty at night and burrowed into a haystack to sleep. As the danger continued, some tried more elaborate options. DeLancey's Cow Boys raided the Van Wart farm at Elmsford so often that Mrs. Van Wart constructed a hut camouflaged as a haystack in which the family could hide during raids, no doubt praying that the raiders didn't pause to set fire to the haystack.[20]

In a war of neighbor versus neighbor, the conflict could become intensely personal. In one example, at the beginning of 1777 a farmer named Thomas Fowler decided to help himself to three cows belonging to his Eastchester neighbor Marcus Christian. Christian caught him in the act and threatened to prosecute, but Fowler promptly denounced Christian to the British as a rebel, Fowler himself, of course, being a loyal subject of the king, or so he said, and the three cows thereby the legitimate spoils of war. The denunciation nearly got Christian hanged by the Queen's Rangers, who dragged him off to face Colonel Robert Rogers in his headquarters in the present-day Valentine-Varian House. Rogers condemned Christian to death, but Christian managed to escape from the house. He never got his cows back.[21]

In addition to physical violence, there was the threat of disease. A moving army was a healthy army, but once the troops settled into camp, even if only for a few weeks, disease would break out, with the danger of it spreading beyond the camp into the civilian population. In the autumn of 1779, an outbreak of "bilious fever" spread throughout the British camps in New York. The diagnosis is imprecise, but it was likely the fever was occasioned by malaria, accompanied by jaundice and nausea, although viral hepatitis or sepsis are also possibilities.[22]

Typhoid could contaminate the local water sources and flea-borne typhus could also infect people outside the camp, but the most feared disease was smallpox. The outbreak of the war accelerated an epidemic of smallpox that began in Boston. Despite Washington's insistence on inoculating his troops, in 1781 an outbreak occurred at the Continental army encampment at New Windsor on the Hudson. A high turnover of personnel brought many non-inoculated men into camp, and the army was unable to keep up with the inoculation program.

A vaccine for smallpox was still a generation away, and the only preventive measure was inoculation. This involved the application of pus from an active patient into a healthy body. For reasons that are still unclear, this induced a milder case of the disease, and while inoculation could still kill people (including two children and a niece of King George), the death rate was dramatically lower than in naturally contracted cases, and the survivors gained a lifelong immunity. While soldiers were inoculated by order, there was no corresponding program for the civilian population, and many private doctors were reluctant to administer it.[23]

Apart from the deadly diseases going around, there was "the itch," or "scabies." Believed to be the consequence of soldiers sleeping on bare ground, it could affect civilians too. It was caused by tiny mites inhabiting unwashed clothing; they burrowed into the skin and caused itching scabs. The more a soldier scratched, the more inflamed it became. Treatments included such things as sulfur-infused soap (always in short supply), a concoction of tar and sulfur applied to the skin or, as a last resort, an application of pig's lard, which hopefully would suffocate the little devils.

The violence, banditry and social disruption caused by the war displaced a lot of people. Some fled from the baleful presence of once-friendly neighbors. Others saw their way of life destroyed as their homes and wheat fields were set ablaze and their livestock driven off to feed one side or the other. Some, wrenched from their place in society, never made it back home.

Beverly Robinson at first sought to remain neutral in the conflict. A merchant from Virginia and a onetime friend of George Washington, he had married into the Philipse family and enjoyed an enviable country estate at the foot of Sugar Loaf Mountain alongside the Hudson across from West Point. He was nevertheless drawn into the war, leaving his riverside estate and joining the British in New York City, where he raised the Loyal American Regiment and became its colonel. Robinson would never return to Beverly House, which became the headquarters of Benedict Arnold. Robinson would act as a go-between facilitating the meeting of Arnold and John André, and after André's capture he would serve as a character witness in a failed attempt to secure André's release. Immigrating to England after the war, Robinson would be short-changed by his own side when the British government awarded him a mere £17,000 for a lost estate valued at £80,000.[24]

One of the more notable individuals displaced by the war was Sarah Bishop. Her origins are uncertain and subject to the embroidery of legend. The likeliest version has it that she was the daughter of a prominent Patriot family on Long Island. When the British occupied Long Island in 1776, the family home was trashed by soldiers, and Sarah was subjected to abuse and possibly sexual assault by a British officer. Traumatized and with her childhood home in ashes, she fled Long Island. She appeared as a homeless wanderer in Ridgefield, Connecticut, in the early years of the war and eventually made her way to North Salem, where she lived a solitary life in what to this day is known as "Sarah Bishop's Cave."

Kind locals would help Sarah out with donations of food, and otherwise she got by through such odd jobs as spinning, knitting or sewing. She would harvest what wild berries, nuts and grapes the mountain had to offer and planted potatoes, cucumbers and beans in her rocky garden, shaded by a few peach trees she managed to plant.[25]

Although she spoke little about herself, Sarah was not antisocial, and as a local eccentric she was more pitied than feared. In ragged clothes most of the time, she would put on a good dress she saved from somewhere to attend church on Sundays, after which she would retire to her cave. Her abode on Long Pond Mountain was hardly commodious, being a rock shelter about four feet high and six feet deep, the entrance protected by a screen of tree branches. In fair weather, she would sit outside perched on "Sarah Bishop's Rock," where passersby would see her gazing in the direction of Long Island. She died in 1809 from hypothermia after being caught in a blizzard and was buried in an unmarked grave at June Cemetery in North Salem. About one hundred years later, a plaque was placed in the cemetery to commemorate Sarah, who by then had become a community legend.

Another legendary Westchester hermit proved to be a Patriot. "Hulda the Witch," or Hulda of Bohemia as she is more properly known, was not a displaced person, at least not by the Revolutionary War. Her origins were even more murky than that of Sarah Bishop, but she was said to have hailed from Bohemia, part of today's Czech Republic, making her a rather exotic character in the Anglo-Dutch community of Tarrytown. Not an accepted part of that community, Hulda lived alone in a small hut outside the town close by Spook Rock, where spectral figures were said to dance in the moonlight.

As the story is told, Hulda was an herbalist who gathered the medicinal bounty of the forest. That, plus her Spook Rock address, was enough for many nervous villagers to aver that she was a witch and therefore best avoided. Hulda took this shunning in stride and would leave offerings of healing herbs on the doorsteps of people she knew to be ill.

When in October 1777 the British landed in Tarrytown on a search-and-destroy mission, the militia turned out to defend their town at the redoubt on Battle Hill overlooking the Old Dutch Church, and Hulda was there too, getting hold of a musket and picking off British soldiers. Hulda proved to be a crack shot, dropping several Redcoats. The startled British focused their fire on Hulda, and she died in a hail of lead.

In the aftermath of the raid, some who had spurned Hulda reconsidered their attitude, especially after her cabin was searched. Among the reputed witch's meager possessions was a well-used Bible, along with a small cache of money and instructions to apply these funds to relieve the needy of Tarrytown. The shamefaced villagers decided that Hulda deserved a Christian burial at the Old Dutch Church, albeit in an unmarked grave by the shadowy north wall of the church.

The legendary Hulda of Bohemia was a Tarrytown hermit who took up arms to defend her neighbors. *Photo by the author.*

Historians point to the lack of documentation of Hulda's story as reason to doubt that she ever existed and note that there is no record of her burial in church archives, nor is the precise location of her grave known in an otherwise well-documented churchyard.[26] Nevertheless, in recent years Hulda has been adopted as a local hero by the residents of Sleepy Hollow. In 2019, the Friends of the Old Dutch Church and Burying Ground funded a headstone for Hulda. Erected in the approximate location of her reputed grave, the stone was carved in painstakingly authentic eighteenth-century style by master carver Robert Carpenter and has become a popular point of interest for visitors to the churchyard, who leave on her tombstone a variety of offerings, including such things as Tootsie Pops and postage stamps.[27]

Hulda is also remembered by a one-woman show, *Hulda: The Other Legend of Sleepy Hollow*, performed by Carla Lynne Hall every October, along with lantern-lit walking tours and campfire stories offered as part of an annual "Hulda's Night" at the Rockefeller State Park Preserve.[28]

Chapter 3

THE YEAR OF THE HANGMAN

The year 1777 would be dubbed the "Year of the Hangman." Numerologists and soothsayers may have seen a portent in its repetition of three sevens, but others saw in it a row of gallows. The British confidently expected them to be bedecked with dead rebels, while the rebels wished the same on the British and their Tory henchmen. Behind these perceptions was a sense that after the inconclusive 1776 campaign, 1777 would be the year of decision. As indeed it proved to be.

In the Neutral Ground, the new year began with an attack on the British fortifications guarding the crossings over the Harlem River and Spuyten Duyvil Creek.

Following his success at the Battle of Princeton, Washington needed to move his army into secure winter quarters. He chose Morristown, New Jersey, which sat in defendable terrain amid the Watchung Mountains, close enough to New York to keep the British on edge and under observation.

An army changing its base is vulnerable, especially if the base, such as the Morristown encampment, hasn't been constructed yet. Washington therefore needed something to distract the British into staying in New York City while he moved into Morristown. He ordered General William Heath to bring his detachment down from the Hudson Highlands and mount an attack on the Kingsbridge fortifications to make it look as if an American attempt to retake New York City was in the offing.

As it were, Heath's move fooled nobody, but the British, still discombobulated from the debacles at Trenton and Princeton, were in no mood for a midwinter march across New Jersey. Nevertheless, Heath's attack got off to a good start, as the British remained clueless until American troops crossed William's Bridge over the Bronx River. Outposts monitoring the Boston Post Road at the Valentine House and the so-called Negro Fort fled without a shot, the men making pell-mell for the safety of Fort Independence, now renamed Fort No. 4.[29]

The initial American success, though, soon ran into a wall of well-manned British defenses. Lacking sufficient troops with which to storm Fort No. 4, Heath tried to bluff his way to victory, issuing a preemptory demand for surrender with a twenty-minute deadline. This was greeted with derision, and British headquarters sent orders for the men to maintain their positions and let the Americans make fools of themselves.

What had been a carefully planned maneuver quickly devolved into a series of uncoordinated cannonades against various parts of the British fortifications until January 24, when the British launched a sortie against their erstwhile besiegers. The Americans fled from the sudden assault. Some took refuge in a redoubt overlooking William's Bridge and served as sort of a rear guard while the rest withdrew across the Bronx River.[30]

The abortive siege of Kingsbridge accomplished its mission of distracting the British long enough for Washington to move his army into Morristown, but Washington took Heath to task for what he saw as a bungled operation, commenting in a private letter to Heath that Heath's summons to surrender "was not only idle, but farcical, and will not fail of turning the laugh exceedingly upon us." A few weeks later, Washington took the opportunity offered by the retirement of General Artemas Ward to transfer Heath to the command of the New England department and placed Alexander McDougall in charge of Westchester and the Hudson Highlands.[31]

While Heath packed his bags, the once-renowned Robert Rogers was on his way out. The British command had been having doubts about Rogers ever since the surprise attack on his encampment at Mamaroneck the previous October. The onetime hero of the French and Indian War was seen as an erratic, none-too-sober loose cannon, and an incident during the siege of Kingsbridge reinforced this perception. On January 13, Rogers sent the Queen's Rangers on a risky and pointless raid into northern Westchester against the Bedford home of Henry Williams, a member of the Provincial Congress. The raid accomplished little, the plunder consisting of such swag as a beaver hat, a smart waistcoat and an officer's sword.

In the meantime, Alexander Innis, General Howe's newly appointed inspector general of Provincial forces, produced a damning report on Rogers

An ill-starred attack on the British Kingsbridge fortifications was launched by General William Heath in January 1777. *Library of Congress.*

and his tatterdemalion Queen's Rangers. "I found the Provincial Corps in very great confusion and disorder," Innis later recalled. "Their conduct in a thousand instances was so flagrant, that I could not hesitate to tell the General, that until a thorough reformation took place, he could expect no service from that battalion."[32]

Rogers was relieved of command, and the Queen's Rangers would find themselves under a new commander who would shape it into an entirely different, and far more lethal, unit.

As if to make up for the shambolic Kingsbridge foray, on March 16 the Americans launched an ambitious foraging raid against the Loyalist haven in Morrisania. The raid achieved surprise, and the raiders made off with grain and cattle, some of which had no doubt been recently stolen from Patriot farmers.

Knowing that the raiders would withdraw up the White Plains Road east of the Bronx River, troops were dispatched from Fort No. 8 to intercept the raiders at Williams Bridge. The Americans, though, had foreseen this response and had left a party of riflemen to keep the British from crossing the bridge. An afternoon-long firefight resulted, but the British were kept on the west bank of the river long enough for the raiding party, with their slow-moving wagons and cattle, to safely proceed up the White Plains Road. Or so they thought.[33]

The sheer brazenness of this raid was too much to be allowed to pass without retaliation, and the Queen's Rangers, now under the temporary command of Major Archibald Campbell, along with a detachment of Hessians, was dispatched to follow the Americans all the way up to their rallying point at the Stephen Ward house in Tuckahoe.

Situated at the twenty-three-mile marker (from New York's city hall), the Ward House was a convenient landmark where the militia could gather. That evening, the troops were gathered there to sort out the plunder and congratulate themselves on a job well done, thinking themselves safe from enemy pursuit. The Rangers and Hessians came upon them by surprise. Captain Samuel Crawford, head of the Scarsdale militia contingent, was about to head for home when the shooting started. In the ensuing fight, he was mortally wounded and would die in British custody several months later.[34]

Major Campbell was also killed, allegedly by Americans who had already offered their surrender, an allegation that would characterize a number of other lethal incidents in the Neutral Ground. The death of Campbell prompted a round of mad firing in which a number of Americans were killed. The British lost at least eight men killed.[35]

The spring of 1777 was a time of uncertainty. With a British invasion under General John Burgoyne moving from Canada down the Champlain Valley, the question was what General Howe in New York would do. Would he strike up the Hudson to link up with Burgoyne? Or would he head south to attack Philadelphia? Washington's spies could give little enlightenment—the plain fact was that Howe hadn't made up his mind yet.

While Howe pondered his options, there were things his army could do to keep the rebels guessing. One was to launch attacks on Continental supply bases in Peekskill and Danbury, Connecticut. These northward movements would keep Washington unclear as to which direction Howe was planning to go, while the destruction of supplies would hamper Washington's army in any event.

The death of Samuel Crawford is commemorated by a monument in Tuckahoe outside the Ward House. *Photo by the author.*

On the afternoon of March 23, a British force of about five hundred troops landed at Lent's Cove and made for Peekskill Landing about a mile and a half to the north. Seeing himself outnumbered by more than two to one, General McDougall destroyed such supplies as he could and made a timely retreat north to Cortlandt. Reinforced by local militia, the next day the Americans came south and engaged the British covering force on what today is known as Fort Hill overlooking Peekskill Landing. The skirmishing caused few casualties to either side but allowed McDougall to claim that he had driven the enemy from Peekskill.

By then the damage had been done, and the Redcoats no longer had any reason to stay around. Apart from what had been destroyed by the retreating Americans, the toll included 400 hogsheads of rum, 100 barrels of flour and salt pork and 130 wagons, along with quantities of sugar, coffee, chocolate and salt, as well as "a great parcel of Smoked Beef and Dried Tongues."[36]

The raid on Peekskill was followed up one month later with an expedition against Danbury, Connecticut. Militia forces, mobilized by Sybil Ludington's legendary ride, were unable to prevent the burning of Danbury and the destruction of the supplies stored there, but they engaged the British at the Battle of Ridgefield.[37]

After a spring and summer of false moves, the issue was decided by the news of Burgoyne's capture of Fort Ticonderoga on July 6. Howe concluded that Burgoyne was doing quite well for himself and had no need of help from the south, so Howe packed up his fleet and set sail for Pennsylvania, with Washington cautiously following by land.

General Henry Clinton was of a different mind, but with barely enough troops to secure New York City, there wasn't much he could do to aid Burgoyne. In the meantime, Burgoyne was running into trouble, and an urgent plea for help convinced Clinton that he had to do something.

The vulnerability of the lower Hudson Valley was no secret to either side. All through 1776, Royal Navy vessels had been prowling the river south of West Point. They took depth soundings, revised their nautical charts and paid little concern to the gunshots of the Westchester and Orange County militias. While British frigates cruised the waters, the American commanders recognized the strategic importance of the navigation bottleneck at West Point and scrambled for ways of denying it to the British.

Early fortifications at Martelaer's Rock (Constitution Island) were soon deemed inadequate, and early in 1777, the newly organized Fifth New York Continental regiment was assigned to fortify a rocky prominence at Popolopen Creek on the western shore just north of Bear Mountain.

Named Fort Montgomery in honor of General Richard Montgomery, who was killed in the doomed assault on Quebec, the fort occupied a strong position overlooking a chain stretched across the Hudson, but General Lord Sterling spotted another projecting prominence to the south. With only

Above: Earthworks on Fort Hill above Peekskill recall a devastating British raid in 1777. *Photo by the author.*

Left: A reconstructed Fort Montgomery looks out over the Hudson River. *Photo by the author.*

a one-acre footprint, the prominence was too small for a major fort, but nevertheless enemy guns mounted on it could threaten Fort Montgomery. A subsidiary fortification was therefore constructed there, named Fort Clinton after the New York State governor and Brigadier General George Clinton. From the river, the "Twin Forts" appeared to be all but unassailable, or so it was thought.[38]

British General Clinton could only spare three thousand men for the expedition, but with canny planning he could capture the Twin Forts and threaten, or even capture, West Point. This might clear the way to sail up the Hudson to link up with Burgoyne at Albany, or at the very least it would draw American forces away from Burgoyne. Clinton wisely chose not to risk his line-of-battle warships against the Twin Forts in a direct assault but instead sent infantry to attack the forts from the less defended landward sides, while smaller British vessels would engage American gunboats on the river.

As a diversionary move to destroy supplies and distract the militia in Westchester, a landing was made at Tarrytown under General and Royal Governor William Tryon. After a brief maneuver into central Westchester, Tryon sailed north to Verplanck and eventually succeeded in destroying the American supply depot at Continental Village in Fishkill. On the way back to the river, he passed through Peekskill and burned whatever buildings were still standing after the March raid.

With the guidance of local Loyalist Beverly Robinson, Clinton landed his main force at Stony Point, marched west around Bear Mountain and came down upon the Twin Forts from the rear. Outnumbering the American defenders two to one, the British captured the forts and inflicted casualties on the Americans of 70 killed, 40 wounded and 240 captured, while British vessels thoroughly mangled the American river flotilla. British casualties, though, were also high, with 40 dead and 150 wounded.

With the forts taken and the river chain broken, the way was clear for British vessels to sail up the Hudson, and Clinton dispatched General John Vaughn with a small force to capture what was then the New York provincial capital in Kingston. The rebel government of New York made a timely evacuation, and the frustrated raiders set Kingston and Esopus ablaze on October 16. The embers of Kingston hadn't cooled when news arrived that Burgoyne had surrendered his army on October 17. There was now no point in leaving his soldiers out on a limb up the Hudson and in danger of an overwhelming assault by victory-enthused Americans charging down from Saratoga, so Clinton withdrew back to Manhattan.[39]

Where grand strategy faltered individual enterprise filled the gaps, and 1777 saw the beginning of a curious waterborne guerrilla conflict known as the "Whaleboat War." Knowing that the British army in New York needed fresh provisions, and that many Westchester farmers were more than willing to trade with the enemy for hard cash, small bands of Patriot raiders began setting out in whaleboats to intercept vessels carrying food to Manhattan.

It was a small-craft counterpart to the privateering war being waged on the broad Atlantic, and it pinched British logistics. Not content with denying turnips to the Redcoats, the rebel boatmen would sometimes aim for more ambitious targets. In one spectacular example, a boat from Darien, Connecticut, intercepted a "market boat" that sailed a regular route from Eastchester to New York. Taking over the small sloop, they approached the *Schuldam*, a British gunboat stationed at the mouth of Eastchester Creek to guard the market boat traffic and overawe the local Patriots.

The crew of the *Schuldam*, thinking that the market sloop had come to sell them cabbages or something, allowed the craft to lay alongside their vessel, whereupon the whaleboat men stormed out of the hold, seized control of the *Schuldam* and set fire to it.

As time went on, Patriot whaleboat men took to raiding Loyalist farmsteads on Long Island, prompting retaliation by Loyalist whaleboat men. Battles were sometimes fought out between competing whaleboat flotillas on the open water, and the raiding of coastal farms in Westchester only added to the growing mayhem.[40]

While the main actions of the war were being fought out in places as far afield as Philadelphia and Saratoga, conditions in the Neutral Ground steadily descended into lawless chaos as freebooters and assorted vigilantes on either side took advantage of the power vacuum. Yet the Year of the Hangman would be seen as a relatively quiet period, as the following summer would bring a renewed upsurge of violence to the Neutral Ground.

Chapter 4

THE WESTCHESTER GUIDES

As the main armies returned to the Hudson Valley in the summer of 1778, they faced a familiar problem: a lack of accurate and detailed maps, particularly of the Neutral Ground. Existing maps of Westchester County were for the most part sketchy depictions showing the main roads linking villages and towns. While these maps were adequate for civilian purposes, they did not show the web of unmapped and unnamed lanes, byways, trails and shortcuts that could be crucial to military operations.[41]

In July 1777, Washington appointed Robert Erskine as geographer and surveyor general to resolve this problem. An ironmaster, professional surveyor and a Fellow of the Royal Society of London, the Scottish-born Erskine was initially tasked with mapping the Hudson Highlands, leaving the Neutral Ground an area where the army depended on the local knowledge provided by a corps of scouts that became known as the Westchester Guides.

Off the main roads, navigating the complicated terrain of Westchester County was no easy task, and the need for local assistance became apparent in the autumn of 1776. Retreating northward, Washington had to send out his chief engineer, Colonel Rufus Putnam, to scout a route by which the army could safely move from Yonkers to White Plains, less than a dozen miles away. Fortunately, once in White Plains, Washington found committed Patriots with the intimate local knowledge that he needed.

Isaac and Cornelius Oakley were the first to step forward. The Oakley Tavern in White Plains had been a gathering place for the rebellious-minded, who discussed the issues of the day while casting a cold eye on the Loyalist

Hatfield Tavern across the street.[42] The Oakleys, however, were a mainly Quaker family, many of whom disapproved of any military participation.

The family nevertheless had their own history of rebellion. The family's Westchester progenitor, Miles Oakley, was said to have served in Oliver Cromwell's Roundheads fighting against the monarchy in the English civil wars of the 1640s. Miles immigrated to Westchester Town shortly after the restoration of King Charles II in 1660, and by the 1770s, the Oakley family were well established in White Plains.[43]

For Isaac and Cornelius, serving as guides rather than regular soldiers may have been a compromise between their religious and patriotic beliefs. They helped get the bedraggled Americans settled into good defensible positions for the Battle of White Plains and later advised their withdrawal north to Fishkill. Together with their cousin James Oakley from Westchester Town, Isaac and Cornelius would serve to the very end of the war.[44]

In January 1777, General Heath blamed the failure of his attack against the British Kingsbridge defenses partly on the lack of accurate knowledge of the terrain. He decided to recruit a full-time corps of "mounted guides" and applied to the Committee of Safety, which furnished eight volunteers. In time, the Westchester Guides, as they came to be known, would enroll more than two dozen men.[45]

Like the Oakleys of White Plains, the Odell family of Greenburgh were tavernkeepers. Their home in the present-day village of Irvington doubled as a wayside inn, situated as it was on the Albany Post Road (today's Broadway). It had briefly served as the headquarters of the Committee of Safety after the British took New York City and, during the British withdrawal from White Plains, had been occupied and looted (despite the efforts of their enslaved servant Caesar).

The Odells also had a rebellious history if family tradition is to be believed. It was said that a relative of theirs, one Samuel Odell, had sailed under the pirate Blackbeard and was wounded in the ultimate battle off North Carolina's Ocracoke Island in 1718. Taken captive, Samuel escaped the hangman by claiming to have been an unwilling buccaneer who was captured by the pirates and forced to fight in their scurvy crew.

The Odells were a widely dispersed clan in Westchester. Some of them would prove to be Loyalists, but the Greenburgh Odells were firmly pro-independence. The six-foot John Odell had volunteered for militia service at the outset of the war, and at the end of 1776, he was recruited by General Heath, along with his cousins Michael and Abraham "Brom" Dyckman, to guide his approach against the British fortifications around Kingsbridge.

The Patriot Odell family maintained a tavern on the Albany Post Road in present-day Irvington. *Library of Congress.*

Brandishing a brace of pistols and riding a dapple-gray horse personally gifted him by Lieutenant Governor Pierre Van Cortlandt, John Odell was renowned for his physical presence and fighting prowess. He was one of the most feared members of the Westchester Guides, and the British posted a £100 reward for his capture.

John's cool head and fighting skills would come in handy when on September 16, 1778, the British launched a surprise attack on an American light infantry company camped at the present-day Oakland Cemetery in Yonkers. Amid the panic and confusion, Odell rallied the men and enabled them to escape the encirclement and get to safety across the Saw Mill River.[46]

Two weeks after the Yonkers fight, John's cousin Isaac Odell helped set the ambush that resulted in the Battle of Edgar's Lane on September 30, 1778. One of three Isaacs serving in the Guides (biblical names were popular then, including another Isaac Odell from Greenburgh), Odell, from Yonkers, bore the curious nickname of "Uck" but was no less respected for it. Thanks in part to Uck's guidance, Edgar's Lane was one of the most spectacular small-unit American victories of the war and a morale-boosting payback for the Stockbridge massacre the month before.

Another renowned guide was Abraham "Brom" Dyckman.[47] After evacuating his family from northern Manhattan, Brom enlisted in the Westchester Militia, and in early 1777, his name came to General Heath's attention as a prospective guide. Coming from the very neighborhood where the Kingsbridge forts were located, Brom was a natural choice to assist the American forces in their attack. Brom and his younger brother Michael joined John Odell to escort General Benjamin Lincoln's supporting column as it moved south from Tarrytown.

The expedition's failure did little to dampen Brom's reputation. Known for his bravery as well as his amiable personality, he was chosen to be part of the permanent corps of Westchester Guides. Brom and his fellow guides tangled so often with James DeLancey's Loyalist raiders that Washington eventually tasked them with taking DeLancey prisoner.

Teaming up with the redoubtable John Odell, Brom made several attempts to nab DeLancey. The wily DeLancey (who seldom accompanied his troops into the field) proved a difficult fellow to catch. Headquartered in the Archer House close to the British Fort No. 8, DeLancey seemed to have a sixth sense that enabled him to elude repeated attempts to capture him. A frustrated Brom Dyckman continued to pursue DeLancey until a final attempt in the spring of 1782 cost him his life.

While not a regular member of the corps of Westchester Guides, Sergeant John Dean of Tarrytown gave valuable service in the Neutral Ground. He and his family had been deeply involved in the Revolution from the beginning: Dean had been part of the crowd that tore down the statue of George III on New York City's Bowling Green on July 9, 1776. He and his older brother William then enlisted in the rebel cause and joined in the assault on Quebec, where William died. Returning home to Westchester, Dean served as a guide in several attacks on James DeLancey's Loyalist haven in Morrisania. These repeated raids irked DeLancey so much that he specifically targeted Dean for capture. Dean was snatched from his Mount Pleasant home in December 1780 but was soon exchanged for a prominent Loyalist captive. Shortly before his capture, Dean had been part of the militia patrol that brought in John André.

When not on regular duty, Dean pursued his own personal war on the Loyalists. On one occasion, he engaged a local Loyalist named Basly in a mounted duel. Basly tried several times to shoot Dean, but Dean dodged the bullets and finally wounded his opponent and knocked him off his horse. The chivalrous Dean then took the gravely injured Tory to a nearby farmhouse, carefully dressed his wounds and thereby saved his life. After the war, the two would meet again and make their peace with each other.[48]

John Dean gained little fame for his role in André's capture (he was inadvertently left out of the initial report of the incident and was added only

Left: Abraham and Isaac "Uck" Odell were two of the most prominent Westchester Guides. *Photo by the author.*

Opposite: Though at first left out of accounts of André's capture, Westchester Guide John Dean's name is inscribed on the Patriot's Monument on Battle Hill at Sleepy Hollow Cemetery. *Photo by the author.*

years after when his wife, Mary, applied for a Revolutionary War widow's pension). His name remains enshrined in the landscape of Westchester. John Dean Rock, a favorite ambush site of his, where he would lie in wait for Tories passing along the Saw Mill River Road, may be found today near the South County Trailway in Pocantico Hills. He is inscribed on the Revolutionary War Soldiers Monument in Sleepy Hollow Cemetery, and his rifle is in the historic firearms collection of the Metropolitan Museum of Art.[49]

The youngest of the Westchester Guides was Andrew Corsa, who was all of nineteen years old when on July 22, 1781, George Washington showed up on his doorstep, seeking Andrew's guidance in pursuing the Grand Reconnaissance. Washington was seeking a route by which he could assault the British on Manhattan Island, and Andrew's local knowledge was invaluable as he guided Washington, Rochambeau and most of the American high command through what today is the southwest part of The Bronx. The chink in the British defenses proved elusive, and at the end of the day, the generals turned their horses northward and dropped Andrew back at the family farm (about where Fordham University is today), where like an AWOL teenager Andrew was confronted by an irate father. His father, Isaac, was a Loyalist whose convictions were so strong that he formally disinherited Andrew for Andrew's services to the rebel cause.

That disinheritance would pose problems later for Andrew, and he profited little from his contributions as a Westchester Guide. Father Isaac kept his ownership of the family farm until after the war, when his lands were confiscated by New York State. Having been disinherited, Andrew had no legal standing with which to contest the seizure or claim ownership

for himself, nor had he the financial resources with which to purchase the property, and consequently he saw the family farm, and his childhood home, pass into the hands of others.

It was a poor reward for a Patriot such as Andrew, but in time he scraped up enough cash and credit to purchase an adjacent property and settled down to a long life as a Westchester farmer. At his Fordham farm, he developed a distinctive pear varietal known as the Corsian Vergaloo, which is still cultivated today. By the time he died at the age of ninety in 1852, Andrew was revered as one of the last veterans of the Revolution.[50]

The British for their part had their own corps of Guides and Pioneers. Organized at the end of 1776, the Guides comprised between 100 and 150 Loyalists, most of whom were from Westchester and the Hudson Valley. Though often providing valuable service in such instances as the Danbury Raid and the Philadelphia Campaign, as well as in the Neutral Ground, the British Guides suffered from mediocre leadership, exacerbated by a succession of five commanders, none of whom remained long enough to put his own stamp on the unit. While he appreciated the dedication of the men, General Clinton would complain about the large number of no-show and do-little officers who made the Guides and Pioneers somewhat less than useful. By contrast, the dedication and intimate local knowledge of the American Westchester Guides would prove crucial as the war in the Neutral Ground intensified in 1778.

Chapter 5

THE BLOODY SUMMER OF 1778

Following the British withdrawal from Philadelphia and the inconclusive Battle of Monmouth, New Jersey, on June 28, 1778, the main British and American forces arrived back in the lower Hudson Valley, for the moment quite out of ideas as to what to do next.

The previous year's campaigns had not gone well for the British. John Burgoyne's invasion down the Champlain Valley had ended in ignominious surrender at Saratoga, while William Howe's capture of Philadelphia had been a hollow triumph. Encouraged by the news of Saratoga, the French entered the war on behalf of the Americans, and in the meantime, Washington used the winter encampment at Valley Forge to reshape his army into something like the professional fighting force he had always wished for.

The British, now under General Henry Clinton, abandoned Philadelphia and, after fighting off Washington's troops at Monmouth, settled back into their Manhattan Island defenses. Clinton's long desire for appointment to the supreme command proved to be a booby prize: with the entry of the French the war had gone global, and the British needed to redeploy soldiers to defend their lucrative Caribbean sugar islands. Clinton no sooner assumed command than the offensive capabilities of his forces were reduced by five thousand troops.

While the contending armies glowered at each other in Pennsylvania and New Jersey, for the Neutral Ground the first half of 1778 was quiet, even leading to some boredom among the American troops guarding the Hudson Highlands. Surgeon James Thatcher found himself installed at a hospital located at the home of Loyalist Beverly Robinson (above present-day Garrison), with few battle casualties demanding his attention. He was unimpressed by the "hideous mountains and dreary forests" that surrounded the place, and for diversion he made the difficult climb up Sugar Loaf Mountain, where he and his friends amused themselves by rocking one of the glacial boulders. Colonel Rufus Putnam did more than that—with some forty men he ascended Sugar Loaf and put his engineering skills to work by dislodging an enormous glacial erratic and watching it tumble down to the Hudson shoreline, where it became known as "Putnam's Rock."[51]

The leisurely days of tumbling boulders ended in July when Washington arrived in the Hudson Valley and ordered a forward perimeter to be set up across central Westchester to keep a wary eye on the British. The general established his headquarters near the front line at the home of Abagail and Jacob Purdy, while his men reoccupied their old positions from the Battle of White Plains nearly two years before. For many it was not a nostalgia trip: Joseph Plumb Martin was horrified to find the unburied bones of Hessian soldiers left at Chatterton Hill.

Confronting each other over the expanse of the Neutral Ground, each army needed to reconnoiter the other, while at the same time preventing the enemy from doing the same. The result would be a series of small unit actions that would become Westchester's most violent summer of the war so far.

James DeLancey had been pursuing his own war up to this point, but now he and his Westchester Refugees were joined by three of the most ruthless Loyalist units: John Graves Simcoe's Queen's Rangers, Andreas Emmerich's Chasseurs and Banastre Tarleton's British Legion.

For the so-called Provincial units supporting the British war effort, 1778 marked a new departure in their role. Previously they had been minor auxiliaries of the Redcoats and Hessians, often detailed to garrison duty or consigned to the rear echelons. With the reductions in troop strength, the British command was forced to increasingly rely on the Loyalists, and ambitious commanders such as Simcoe and Tarleton grasped the opportunity to shape their commands into independent units that would strike deep into enemy territory.

The twenty-six-year-old John Graves Simcoe was the son of a Royal Navy captain, and his middle name honored another navy captain, Samuel Graves. Despite these oceanic namesakes, Simcoe opted for a career in the British army and served as a captain of the First Battalion of Grenadiers. Shortly after the Battle of Germantown, he was appointed commander of

Led by John Graves Simcoe, the Queen's Rangers were a powerful Loyalist force in the Neutral Ground. *Library of Congress.*

the Queen's Rangers on October 15, 1777, and given the rank of major. Simcoe had a reputation for being humorless and was a devoted student of military theory, unlike many of his fellow officers.

Feeling the frustrations of a stalemated war, Simcoe was determined to pursue an aggressive policy in the Neutral Ground, with the enthusiastic support of Banastre Tarleton, Andreas Emmerich and James DeLancey. For Simcoe, however, actions had to be undertaken with a particular object in mind rather than risking his men's lives in aimless troublemaking. Nor was he bloodthirsty, preferring to take prisoners rather than killing the enemy.

Unlike a corpse lying on the ground, a prisoner could be swapped for a British soldier and might provide a useful bit of information in the meantime. With this in mind, Simcoe saw to it that prisoners were treated reasonably well. Against the common practice of the time, he forbade his men from robbing prisoners of their personal effects.

The Queen's Rangers that Simcoe led were a far cry from the dispirited band that Robert Rogers had left two years before. A tough disciplinarian, Simcoe had little regard for the individualistic frontiersmen who formed the legendary Rangers of the previous war, and he made it clear that the reformed Queen's Rangers would be a cohesive force that would fight as a unit. A succession of commanders who followed Rogers had gotten the Rangers to trade in their buckskins and linen hunting shirts for smartly styled green uniforms. The Rangers arrived in Westchester sporting tall brimless hats embellished with a silver crescent moon. Following a friendly fire incident in Pennsylvania earlier that year, Simcoe ordered the new headgear to distinguish his men from the green-clad American dragoons.[52]

Simcoe would have preferred to have the men outfitted in the Regulars' royal red livery, but as a Loyalist unit, green would be their assigned color. He made the best of it, though, pointing out that green would present less of a target in the woods, and as the vegetable dye faded through the year, it would blend in with the fading foliage of the advancing season.

Along with the stylish uniforms, Simcoe saw to it that his men were equipped with new and top-of-the-line weaponry. The .63-caliber Pattern 1776 Infantry Rifle was similar to the rifle used by the Hessian Jaegers. Its short length made it easily deployable by either foot soldiers in thick woods or by men on horseback, and while its maximum accurate range was only two hundred yards, it was more than adequate for the kind of close-in fighting Simcoe had in mind.[53]

Simcoe's efforts paid off, and the Queen's Rangers distinguished themselves in the 1777 campaign. Now seasoned veterans, the Queen's Rangers arrived in Westchester ready and eager to carry the war to the rebels.

Simcoe was joined in Westchester by the young Banastre Tarleton. "Dashing" was an apt description of the twenty-four-year-old cavalryman. The son of a well-to-do London merchant, Tarleton managed to squander most of his inheritance before dropping the study of law and purchasing a commission in a cavalry unit. He quickly discovered that he was a better horse soldier than a lawyer. Joining the American war, he soon gained prominence by capturing General Charles Lee in December 1776. By 1778, he was in command of a new Loyalist force named the British Legion.[54]

The dashing Banastre Tarleton gained notoriety for burning Pound Ridge. *Library of Congress.*

Like Simcoe, Banastre Tarleton inherited a British Legion composed of a mishmash of Loyalists and rebel deserters.[55] It had originally been organized in Philadelphia as the Caledonian Legion recruited from Pennsylvania's Scottish community.[56] It also absorbed the leftovers of the oddly named Royal American Reformers, organized by the turncoat Rudolphus Ritzema to attract fellow American defectors back to the royal cause.

Setting aside his combative instincts for the time being, Tarleton spent the early part of 1778 drilling this unlikely conglomeration into a disciplined fighting force. To enhance his unit's identity and morale, Tarleton modified the existing dragoon helmet into what became known as the Tarleton Helmet: a stiff leather helmet topped off with an eye-catching bearskin plume with swan feather and leopard skin accents. "Ban," as he was known, drove his men hard, but he was a popular commander for all that. The British Legion arrived in Westchester imbued with their commander's aggressive spirit.

Joining the stern Simcoe and the dashing Tarleton was the Hessian Andreas Emmerich.[57] Arriving in America as a captain, in August 1777 Emmerich was authorized to raise his own rifle company. Emmerich's Chasseurs, as they were known, distinguished themselves in Henry Clinton's brief offensive up the Hudson Valley in October 1777 but otherwise were left to guard the Kingsbridge fortifications. Lobbying on Emmerich's part gained him a promotion to lieutenant colonel, with the go-ahead to expand his small rifle company into a mixed force composed of riflemen, light infantrymen and dragoons. Hoping to draw a large number of prospective recruits from which he could cherry-pick the best men, Emmerich offered a whopping signing bounty of three guineas, paid out of his own pocket. Their uniforms followed the green-and-white livery of Loyalist units, topped off with tricorn hats.

By the time Simcoe and Tarleton arrived, Emmerich's men had already gained considerable experience patrolling the Neutral Ground. In addition to patrols, Emmerich gathered intelligence through what he called "secret service work," the details of which have remained secret to this day.

Emmerich trained his men well and impressed on them the need to be prepared for any contingency. In one amusing incident, a group of Chasseurs were bathing at Spuyten Duyvil when word came of an enemy approach. Without hesitation, the men leaped out of the water, grabbed their muskets and took up defensive positions butt naked. Rather than chastise his men for being out of uniform, Emmerich applauded their alacrity and gave them a cash reward.[58]

However feared and effective, Emmerich's Chasseurs would prove to be a short-lived unit. Tensions among the officers built up over the summer of 1778, resulting in a divided command and a near mutiny. Emmerich himself was the divisive factor, with about half his officers supporting him and half bitterly alienated. These tensions impacted the men, and by the end of the year, the demoralized rank and file were deserting in increasing numbers. Contentions grew to such a point that in early 1779, General Henry Clinton decided to break up the troubled Chasseurs and reassign the men to other Loyalist units. Left with no soldiers to command, Andreas Emmerich was hung out to dry, while Simcoe and Tarleton went on to new heights of glory and notoriety.[59]

For both sides, one of the takeaways of the 1776 campaign was that they were deficient in cavalry. Armies needed cavalry, not so much for glorious saber charges but for such day-to-day tasks as guarding flanks on the battlefield, securing lines of communications and scouting.

An infantryman by nature, Washington at first hadn't appreciated the army's need for cavalry, but when the Fifth Connecticut Light Horse Militia joined his army shortly after the Battle of White Plains, he took the opportunity to authorize Colonel Elisha Sheldon to organize a corps of cavalry, using the Fifth Connecticut as its core.

Casually referred to as "Sheldon's Horse," the Second Continental Light Dragoons would be a mainstay of American defenses in the Neutral Ground. Light Dragoons were distinguished by riding smaller, more nimble horses as opposed to the heavy warhorses of the regular dragoons. Equipped with a sword-denting brass helmet topped off with a blade-repelling horsehair crest and armed with pistols, sword and a short-barreled musket (or an old-fashioned blunderbuss), the Light Dragoons could fight on foot or on horseback as the situation demanded.

Arriving in Westchester after service in Pennsylvania and New York's Schoharie Valley, the Dragoons assumed patrolling, security and courier services. They made their presence known in a sharp action against the Queen's Rangers on Clapp's Tavern Road along the Byram River in Rye on October 7, 1778. The Dragoons took the worst of it, losing six men captured in the brief encounter, but it let Simcoe know that there was now a professional force opposing him.

Guarding the western side of Westchester was a colorful unit known as Armand's Legion. Its commander, Colonel Charles Armand Tuffin, Marquis de la Rouërie, had a swashbuckling backstory. Hailing from the Atlantic-facing country of Brittany, Charles had served in the elite Garde de Corps of King Louis XVI until he wounded a cousin of the king in a duel. Faced with imprisonment in the Bastille, he took ship to America to volunteer his services with the American rebels. Dodging capture by a British warship in the Chesapeake, he and his valet literally jumped ship and swam ashore to make their sopping way to Philadelphia.[60]

Perhaps finding the name Tuffin difficult for the Americans to pronounce (to say nothing of Rouërie), he let himself be known as Colonel Armand, and on June 25, 1778, he took command of a unit of foreign volunteers titled the Free and Independent Chasseurs, more familiarly dubbed Armand's Legion. Their time in the Neutral Ground would be brief. In August 1778, the Legion was transferred from the Department of the Highlands to the main American army, in which they would go on to compile an impressive war record.

Another key American unit patrolling the Neutral Ground was the Stockbridge Indian Company, drawn primarily from the Wappinger people of the eastern Hudson Valley. Wappinger men had served the British in the French and Indian War only to have their land stolen from beneath their feet by the ever-acquisitive Philipse family, with the connivance of New York's royal governor and the approval of the Board of Trade in London. The much-diminished Wappinger tribe migrated to the Christian Indian community at Stockbridge, Massachusetts, bearing an abiding hatred of the Philipses and the royalist government.

It thus took little persuasion to attract the Wappingers to the American cause. Led by the sachem Daniel Ninham and his son Abraham, a Stockbridge militia company composed of Wappingers and Mahicans reported for duty at the Siege of Boston and took part in the Battle of Bunker Hill.[61]

Though small in numbers, the aggressive spirit of the Stockbridge Indians, coupled with their hunting and woodcraft skills, quickly made them a valued component of the American forces and a first-class nuisance to the British.

Prowling the Neutral Ground, in early August 1778 they nearly captured Emmerich in a chance encounter. On August 20, they ambushed and inflicted a severe defeat on a detachment of Emmerich's Chasseurs, a success that sealed their fate. Exasperated at the news from Westchester, Henry Clinton directed that Simcoe, Tarleton and Emmerich, together with DeLancey's raiders, join forces to put down these troublesome Indians once and for all.

Placed in overall command of this amalgamated force, Simcoe on August 31 carefully plotted an ambush, knowing that the Stockbridge men tended to travel the high ground west of the Bronx River along the Mile Square Road (today's Van Cortlandt Park East). Attacking what they thought was a detachment of Queen's Rangers, the Stockbridge men found

Opposite: Commemorated by a new sculpture, Daniel Ninham led his Wappinger scouts in service of the American cause. *Courtesy of Michael Keropian, Keropian Sculpture LLC.*

Above: A monument at Van Cortlandt Park commemorates the 1778 Stockbridge Massacre. *Photo by the author.*

themselves caught between the converging forces of Tarleton, Emmerich and DeLancey. His son Abraham dead, the elderly Daniel Ninham stayed behind to cover the retreat of his surviving men, crying out, "I am old, and can die here." Despite Simcoe's grudging admission that "the Indians fought most gallantly," no quarter was given, and seventeen Stockbridge men soon lay dead in what today is Van Cortlandt Park.[62]

Simcoe's force rode away and left the dead and wounded on the field. The nearby Devoe family took in the wounded, but by the time they sought out the dead, wild animals (and perhaps the family dogs) had gotten to the corpses. The Devoes buried the remains in a nearby spot known as "Indian Field" to this day.[63]

Following up on his success against the Stockbridge Indians, on September 16 Simcoe launched a surprise attack on Gist's Additional Continental Regiment posted on Babcock's Hill, a ridge overlooking the Hudson north of Yonkers. This curiously named unit was recruited in Virginia and, under the command of veteran frontiersman Colonel Nathaniel Gist, was intended to serve as scouts. The Virginia men, though, were new to the area and perhaps unaware of the vulnerability of their position so close to the British lines.[64]

Assisted by detachments of Emmerich's Chasseurs and DeLancey's Refugees, Simcoe got into the rear of Gist's men before launching a converging attack. Taken by surprise, Gist's men were routed, and the colonel himself reportedly was caught literally with his pants down and fled the scene half-dressed.

Less than a mile away, Banastre Tarleton launched his own surprise attack against an American detachment located on an adjoining hill that today is Oakland Cemetery. Again the surprise was complete, but the Americans had the presence of mind to fall back into a patch of thick woods, where Tarleton's horses could not go. Luckily, the Westchester Guide John Odell was among them that morning. Odell rallied the men and led them through the woods and across the Saw Mill River, where they could link up with Colonel Gist's retreating troops. It was a good morning's work for Simcoe and Tarleton, but their string of victories would soon invite retaliation.

The British rampage in Westchester was matched by a notably sanguinary incident just across the Hudson. On the night of September 27–28, a detachment of the Third Continental Dragoons was quartered in farmhouses and barns near present-day River Vale, New Jersey, just south of Tappan. Like Gist's regiment, "Lady Washington's Dragoons," as they were known, were Virginia men and new to the area.

Around midnight, they were struck by an overwhelming surprise attack by a mixed force of British under the command of Major General Charles Grey. "No Flint Grey" had gained his nickname the previous summer with a surprise midnight bayonet-only assault on an encampment of Anthony Wayne's troops at Paoli, Pennsylvania. Repeating the "Paoli Massacre," Grey ordered his men to go in with their bayonets, resulting in 69 out of 116 Dragoons killed, wounded or captured. Among the captured was the wounded Colonel Baylor.[65]

The actions of 1778 often had as much to do with seizing food as harassing the enemy. While much is made of the starving Continentals, the British had nutritional challenges of their own. Provisions had to be shipped three thousand miles across the Atlantic, and whatever wasn't spoiled (or sunk) might be captured by American privateers, leaving diminished supplies to arrive at British-held ports. Fresh food, as well as horse fodder and firewood, had to be locally sourced, either paid for with the king's shillings or confiscated at gunpoint. Westchester at this time was a wheat-growing area, and this meant that the harvest season from August to November was an especially active raiding time.[66]

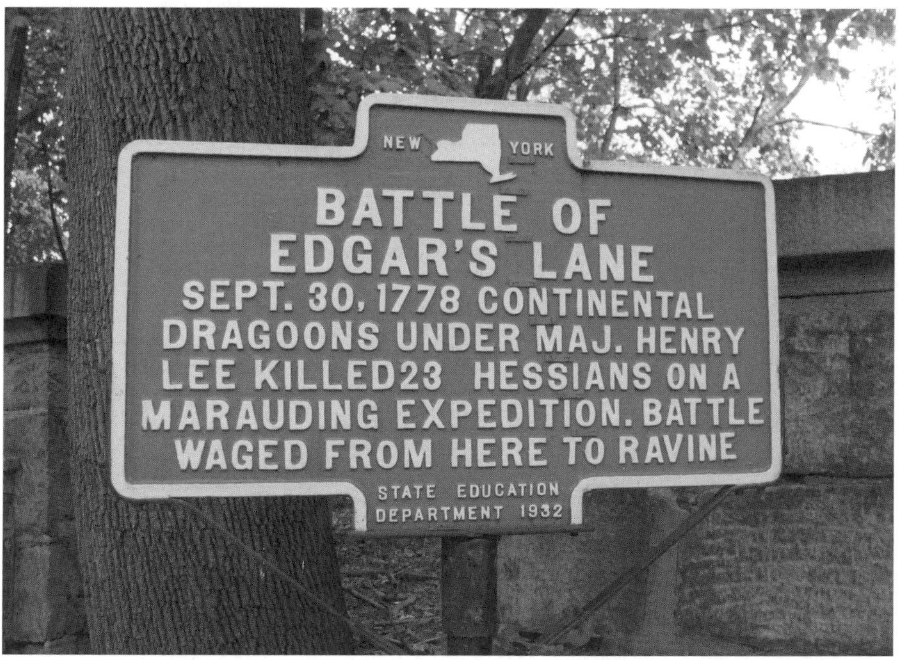

An American ambush at Edgar's Lane in present-day Hastings inflicted a severe defeat on the Hessians. *Photo by the author.*

As the summer of 1778 faded into autumn, a timely tip-off led to the Battle of Edgar's Lane, one of the most successful small-unit actions of the war for the beleaguered Americans. On September 30, word came to Dobbs Ferry that a force of Hessian infantry and cavalry was heading up the Albany Post Road. The four horsemen of the Neutral Ground—Simcoe, Tarleton, Emmerich and DeLancey—had been having a splendid summer, but the Americans now had a star player of their own: Major Henry Lee III, better known as "Light-Horse Harry."[67]

If plodding infantry thought that all cavalrymen were half-mad, Harry Lee was a bit madder than most. His undaunted courage and ruthless energy made him an American counterpart of Banastre Tarleton, and while Lee never gained the deadly notoriety of Tarleton, he had his moments of excess. On one occasion, he ordered an executed deserter decapitated and his head stuck on a pole, earning a reprimand from Washington. His capture of Paulus Hook in 1779 won him both a gold medal and a court-martial brought by disgruntled fellow officers. Toward the end of the war in North Carolina, he turned an accidental encounter with Loyalist militia into what became known as "Pyle's Massacre." Placed in command of a three-company detachment in 1778, Lee was assigned to maintain security in the Neutral Ground.

Lee's unit was among the troops bivouacked at Dobbs Ferry when news came of the enemy's approach. The destination of the Hessian force was uncertain, but Isaac "Uck" Odell knew the local terrain and advised the American commanders of an excellent spot for an ambush along the Albany Post Road.

Then as now, the Albany Post Road was a major north–south thoroughfare. Local farmer Peter Post kept a tavern at the crest of a rise of ground, which, combined with a nearby blacksmith shop, made it an inviting place to pause and ask for directions. Coming down from Dobbs Ferry but not knowing if he was in time to intercept the enemy, Uck Odell popped in to ask Post if he had seen any Hessians go by. Post replied he hadn't, and a relieved Odell turned back to get the Americans positioned for an ambush.

Odell chose his ground well. North of Peter Post's hilltop tavern, the road dipped sharply down, passing a rise of ground to the immediate east, broken by a farm lane perpendicular to the road on the eastern side. The area was still partly wooded, obscuring the view to riders approaching from the south.

The Hessians showed up not long after. As often happens on a long, tedious road march, the men tended to get strung out. The ever-impatient cavalry under Lieutenant Balthasar Mertz cantered ahead and created an exploitable gap in the column as the rear infantry company struggled to catch up. This would create a disaster as the riders descended the hill and drew abreast of the farm lane.

Springing out from the high ground of today's Zinsser Park, American infantry clambered down and blocked the cavalry's way forward, while Light-Horse Harry Lee bounded from the farm lane and swung into the Hessians from the rear. The action was fierce, and in minutes most of Mertz's small detachment were dead or captured. Among the captives was Lieutenant Mertz, severely wounded by a sword blow that severed his nose. The chivalrous Harry Lee returned the heavily bandaged Mertz to the care of the British.[68]

While Light-Horse Harry's men slashed at the cavalry, the forward portion of the Hessian infantry found themselves threatened with encirclement from a combined infantry and cavalry force. Outnumbered and unable to simultaneously defend themselves against both cavalry and infantry, the men made a break for it, fleeing downhill to the Hudson across a set of ravines. Meanwhile, the rear echelon of infantry extricated themselves from the action and retreated down the Albany Post Road.

As many as twenty-eight Hessians lay dead, ample payback for the Stockbridge and Baylor massacres. Viewing the scene shortly after, Hessian Captain Johann Ewald was shocked at the mutilations produced by the sword blows, testimony to the fury with which Lee's men attacked.

The angry and embarrassed Hessians blamed Peter Post for ratting them out to the Americans, or at the very least for not alerting them to the ambush he knew was being set up for them. Shortly after the battle, a gang of irate Jaegers beat Post up and left him for dead on the floor of his tavern. Post nevertheless survived the beating and lived to become a prominent figure in what became the town of Hastings-on-Hudson.[69]

The Neutral Ground of Westchester County was not the only place where partisan fighting and neighbor-on-neighbor violence flared in that violent summer of 1778. Upstate New York's Mohawk Valley was the scene of especially vicious fighting between Patriot American settlers and Loyalist raiders who joined with Seneca, Cayuga and Mohawk fighters who had come out on the British side. The killings culminated with the Cherry Valley massacre on November 11, 1778. Northern New Jersey suffered its own Neutral Ground centered on the Hackensack River Valley, where the "Jersey Dutch" farmers found themselves caught between the contending forces. Within Westchester itself, neighborly contentions grew into what is sometimes referred to as the Saw Mill Valley War.

A series of informational signboards by the Revolutionary Hastings committee of the Hastings Historical Society explain in detail the Battle of Edgar's Lane. *Photo by the author.*

While the fighting raged in the Neutral Ground, the summer of 1778 saw two notable courts-martial held in the White Plains area.

A controversial figure to this day, General Charles Lee was second in command of the American army at the Battle of White Plains in 1776, only to be captured by Banastre Tarleton six weeks later. Exchanged and returned to command, Lee's handling of the American forward echelon at the Battle of Monmouth on June 30, 1778, resulted in a precipitate retreat that nearly lost the battle. The acerbic tone of his subsequent letters to Washington resulted in charges of ordering an unnecessary and unauthorized retreat in the face of the enemy, as well as disrespect to the commander in chief.

The resulting court-martial was something of a traveling road show held in different places as the army moved north from New Jersey, and the final sessions were held at the North Castle house of Ann Fisher Miller, who had been Lee's involuntary hostess during the Battle of White Plains. In the end, the court convicted Lee of disrespect to Washington, but Lee, expecting a full acquittal, resigned his commission and stalked off to his farm in western Virginia.

Shortly after Charles Lee departed, a court-martial was convened to consider charges against General Arthur St. Clair for his retreat from Fort Ticonderoga on July 5, 1777. Ann Fisher Miller was spared the inconvenience of hosting another high-profile court-martial, and instead the trial was held at various locations in the North Castle area. St. Clair was exonerated of all charges and ended the war as an aide-de-camp to George Washington.[70]

The mayhem in the Neutral Ground continued through the autumn. In December, a band of twenty-five of DeLancey's men commanded by Major Mansfield Bearmore rode all the way up to Joseph Young's house near the Croton River, where they stormed the house. Killing two Americans, they took prisoner Daniel Williams and twelve of his Skinners. One of the most notorious leaders of the pro-American Skinners, Williams had been making trouble for what Loyalists still remained in the Neutral Ground, prompting DeLancey to target him for taking out. Williams's band had the day before captured four of DeLancey's men, whom Bearmore liberated while reclaiming some livestock that the Cow Boys had taken and which had been stolen in turn by the Skinners.[71]

In Westchester, the violent year of 1778 finished on Christmas Day with one more notable Loyalist raid. Perhaps thinking that people would be distracted by the holiday, DeLancey's men planned an ambitious double strike against Philipse Manor and North Castle. Christmas, though, was not then the major holiday it would later become, especially not to the Presbyterian Patriots of the area. Instead of sleeping off turkey dinners, in the wake of Bearmore's attack on Young's house people were awake and alert. The raid produced no Yuletide joy for James DeLancey: a prompt turnout by the Westchester militia foiled the Tories, all of whom were killed or captured.

Chapter 6

THE BURNING OF BEDFORD

A reconstructed soldiers' hut behind the Dyckman Farmhouse Museum in northern Manhattan was witness to a shift in British strategy. Built to house eight soldiers, it was one of sixty huts that formed a single Hessian encampment on the farm where Brom Dyckman grew up. Working steps ahead of real estate developers in the early twentieth century, amateur archaeologists Reginald Pelham Bolton and William Louis Calver turned up artifacts from multiple Hessian encampments throughout the hills of northern Manhattan. Taken together, these huts and artifacts tell a tale of declining British fortunes.

The huts and artifacts are evidence of how General Henry Clinton deployed his reduced forces after 1778. The all but irreplaceable British Redcoats were now too valuable to be frittered away in minor skirmishes and backroad donnybrooks, so they were quartered close to the city on lower Manhattan, reserved for serious strategic actions. The more expendable Hessians were encamped on the northern stem of the island, where they would absorb the initial blow of an American attempt to storm Manhattan, something Clinton was always on guard against. It was also wise to keep the Hessians well apart from the British soldiers, as their mutual disdain could easily erupt into disruptive fights.

Clinton further economized his forces by withdrawing from the complex of forts and redoubts that guarded the Kingsbridge crossings on the mainland side of the Harlem River. These forts had been inherited from the retreating Americans in 1776, and not all of them were well sited or useful

Placed in command of the Westchester lines, the young American colonel Aaron Burr marked his twenty-third birthday by burning James DeLancey's blockhouse in West Farms. *Library of Congress.*

to Clinton's purposes. Clinton would retain the pontoon bridgehead of Fort No. 8; otherwise, the consolidation of his defenses would free up soldiers for more mobile operations. The pullback would be carried out over the summer and autumn of 1779, and in the meantime, Clinton relied on Loyalist commanders such as Simcoe and Tarleton to make the Neutral Ground a no-go area for rebel forces. In this they had not been entirely successful, as would be seen when in the first weeks of 1779 a new commander took charge of the forward American lines above White Plains.

The twenty-three-year-old Colonel Aaron Burr was not a man to be trifled with, despite his youth and short (five-foot-six) stature. A veteran of the Canadian campaign, as well as the Battles of White Plains and Monmouth, Burr had a reputation as an energetic field commander and firm disciplinarian. It was said that he had struck a mutineer's arm off with his sword, and although there is no record of this unlikely incident taking place, the legend helped keep the men in line.

Reviewing the situation in the Neutral Ground from his headquarters in Joseph Young's house in Greenburgh, Burr focused his ire on James DeLancey, whose Loyalist Cow Boys had been plundering farmsteads along the Bronx River Valley for the past two years. At West Farms, a substantial log blockhouse guarded a bridge over the Bronx River. It was the southernmost crossing of the Bronx River, situated at present-day 179th Street, between the deep millponds of West Farms and the point where the river widened into an unfordable saltwater estuary. The bridge was also the likely entryway for rebel raiders attacking the Loyalist settlement in Morrisania, as they would usually head down the east side of the Bronx River to avoid interference from British troops stationed at Kingsbridge or Fort No. 8.

In the eighteenth century, midnight assaults were rare events, and armies seldom operated in the dead of winter. After suffering heat stroke at the Battle of Monmouth, Burr may have found the winter chill of Westchester a refreshing respite. Determined to show DeLancey that there was a new force to be reckoned with in the Neutral Ground, shortly after his twenty-third birthday (February 6) Burr organized a strike force to take out the West Farms blockhouse. He gathered a collection of earthenware vessels that he filled with lamp oil and set out just after sundown with his handpicked force.

Heading down the White Plains Road and across the bridge, they arrived at the blockhouse. Wasting no time on surrender negotiations, the raiders tossed their oil pots through the open gun ports, followed by flaming torches that quickly set the blockhouse ablaze. The startled garrison tumbled out of their beds and rushed out the door to surrender. The action was over in minutes. Burr hurried his men and prisoners back up the White Plains Road as the blockhouse burned to the ground. Incredibly, nobody was killed or injured in the fiery assault, and for the young colonel it was a heck of a birthday party.[72]

The destruction of his blockhouse put DeLancey on notice that he had a new, aggressive American commander to contend with. Finding the Neutral Ground to be "a disgraceful scene of plunder and sometimes murder," Burr took forceful steps to turn things around. With fewer than three hundred full-time soldiers, he made the most of what he had. He instituted a system of guard posts across central Westchester and changed their locations regularly to keep the enemy guessing. To keep the sentries on their toes, Colonel Burr personally inspected the posts every night. The guard posts were backed up by both mounted and foot patrols.

The observations of these patrols were gathered to produce sketch maps of the area's terrain and watercourses, useful for determining the directions trouble might come from and places where ambushes might be laid. Burr also organized a network of spies and informants, although his lifelong habit of committing little to paper means that we know next to nothing about who these people were or what useful information they might have provided.[73]

Burr's raid marked a turning point in the partisan war in the Neutral Ground. Although DeLancey's Cow Boys would continue to mount raids right to the very end of the war, they would never again be secure in their Tory stronghold, and American raiders would become increasingly brazen in their retaliatory strikes against West Farms. Burr's command in Westchester, though, would be brief. The lingering effects of his Monmouth heat stroke coupled with the manic energy with which he pursued his new assignment affected his health, prompting him to resign his commission in March 1779.[74]

With Burr out of the picture, the British soon sprang back. A raid led by British General William Tryon on March 25, 1779, created a local legend.

General Israel Putnam made a legendary escape from British raiders who surprised him at Horse Neck (present-day Greenwich, Connecticut). *Library of Congress.*

The target was Horse Neck (today's Greenwich) just over the Connecticut border in Fairfield County. Horse Neck was the site of salt pans, where salt was evaporated from the waters of Long Island Sound. Salt was a valuable commodity in those pre-refrigeration days, and the destruction of the Horse Neck salt pans would be a significant blow to the logistics of Washington's army.

General Israel Putnam was in command in the area. Surprised at his quarters at Knapp's Tavern, it was said that he escaped the British by galloping his horse down a long flight of one hundred stone steps cut into a hillside in order to get to Stamford and turn out the militia. Generations of practical jokers have known how difficult it is to lead a horse down a staircase, and the pursuing British dragoons wisely chose not to follow.

The tale of Putnam's escape added another legend to a man who had already gathered a few legends about him. True or not, the incident is commemorated by a dramatic statue in Putnam Memorial State Park in nearby Redding, Connecticut.

While military units and bands of partisans and bandits crisscrossed the Neutral Ground, the conflict could sometimes be intensely personal. In Tarrytown, the prosperous farmer Nathaniel Underhill was an outspoken Loyalist whose stinginess made him unpopular with his neighbors. In particular there was ill feeling between him and Isaac Martling, which may have predated the war but was nevertheless inflamed by their political divergences.[75] The Patriot Isaac was a veteran who had lost an arm in the French and Indian War, but that didn't stop him from gathering an enthusiastic mob to teach his ungenerous neighbor a lesson. Invading Underhill's farmstead, they hung Underhill by his heels from a beam in his barn and stuffed his mouth with his own grain.

Underhill was otherwise uninjured, but the humiliation prompted him to plan a harsh payback. On May 26, 1779, he caught up with Martling as Martling was hauling a bucket of well water with his one arm. Killing Martling with his sword, Underhill fled the scene, and nobody knew where he went or what became of him.

In view of the political contentions that underlay the killing, the slain Isaac became known as "Isaac the Martyr" and the first murder victim in the heretofore peaceful village of Tarrytown. His original tombstone in the Old Dutch Churchyard baldly stated that he was "inhumanly slain by Nathanial Underhill," and the sandstone marker is said to have been broken by an enraged member of Underhill's family.[76]

While such individual slayings made little impact on the broader course of the war, Banastre Tarleton planned a daring strike that he hoped would be his coup of the year.

Henry Clinton wanted some action staged in Westchester to distract the Americans from his seizure of Verplanck and Stony Point, and Banastre Tarleton was happy to oblige. In the far northern portion of Westchester County, the small hamlet of Pound Ridge was a gathering point for the Westchester militia commanded by Major Ebenezer Lockwood as well as Sheldon's Second American Dragoons. Although Pound Ridge itself was of negligible importance, the capture of Lockwood, Sheldon or, best of all, Sheldon's adjutant Benjamin Tallmadge would hamper American operations in the Neutral Ground and make Tarleton's career.

As Tarleton gathered his Legion in West Farms, word of a big operation planned for Pound Ridge leaked out and was overheard by the American spy Luther Kinnicutt. Although he didn't know the exact date of the strike,

Kinnicutt sensed that it was imminent. There was no time to send word north through the usual channels, so Kinnicutt took the risk of slipping out of West Farms and making his way the about twenty-five miles to Pound Ridge. Kinnicutt arrived in Pound Ridge in time to spread the alarm, but the lack of a date prompted no urgent preparations other than sending out patrols to watch the roads.[77]

It was July 2, 1779, and Tarleton was having fog-of-war problems. Back then, Pound Ridge was a tiny place in a heavily wooded and lightly populated corner of Westchester. The British Legion got lost, and passing through the village of Bedford, they were fired on by some militiamen, which finally alerted the Americans that something was up. Not stopping to deal with the annoying militia, Tarleton pressed on and asked for directions from a farmer named John Crawford. Crawford himself was a Loyalist, but since he wasn't too clear on where Pound Ridge was, he either gave Tarleton bad directions or Tarleton misunderstood him. In any event, it resulted in a time-consuming diversion that cost Tarleton what little remained of the element of surprise.[78]

Bypassing a hastily organized militia ambush, Tarleton finally arrived in Pound Ridge to collide with the American dragoons as they were getting into formation. Slammed by the momentum of Tarleton's charge, the dragoons retreated and were chased by Tarleton's men for several miles.

With the targets of his raid dispersed for the time being, Tarleton turned his attention to the hamlet of Pound Ridge. Having failed to capture or kill Ebenezer Lockwood, Tarleton was about to set fire to his house, only to be dissuaded for the moment by surgeons treating wounded men inside. It proved to be a fortuitous delay. Searching the house, Tarleton came upon the unit flag of the Second Dragoons, a tremendous trophy. Better still, Benjamin Tallmadge had in his haste left behind a satchel of his papers. Tarleton scooped up the satchel for later examination and set fire to the Presbyterian church and, with the wounded removed, the Lockwood house as well. With American militia arriving from all over and taking up ambush positions behind trees and stone walls, Tarleton decided not to linger, hightailing it back to West Farms.[79]

Banastre Tarleton liked setting buildings on fire. It added a dramatic finale to his raids and left a lasting reminder of the consequences of defying the king. He wanted to set fire to Bedford in retaliation for the potshots earlier that day, but with the enraged militia pressing close behind, he thought it best to leave Bedford for another day. He did, though, take time out to set fire to the Crawford farmhouse in return for the bad directions that Tarleton assumed had been given to him on purpose.

As the tired troopers returned to West Farms, Banastre Tarleton's big raid felt like a flop until he had a look at that satchel he picked up in Pound Ridge. Benjamin Tallmadge did double duty as Washington's intelligence officer, and the contents of his lost satchel revealed an intelligence coup that nearly cost the life of an American agent.

Among the papers was a communication from a spy identified only as "E.H." On the paper was a note from George Washington advising that the recipient "believe all that E.H. tells you." It was a rare endorsement from Washington, who tended to be a bit skeptical of spy reports, and it meant that E.H. was a valued asset. The question was who was this E.H.?

Back in New York City, Henry Clinton wanted to know who E.H. was. His counterintelligence operatives had had their eye on Elisha Holmes, who lived uptown near the Bowery. Holmes was hauled in and questioned by General Clinton. Keeping his cool, Holmes examined the paper and claimed that he recognized the handwriting as that of Elijah Hadden, a fellow spy whose initials matched but who, as chance would have it, had been hanged as a spy the day before. Clinton was convinced by this explanation, and as there was as yet no evidence against him, Elisha Holmes was spared the noose for the time being.[80]

The burning that the pyrotechnic Tarleton became most famous for was ironically one he didn't commit. The village of Bedford had nevertheless been marked for destruction, and on July 11, a force of four hundred men led by Lieutenant Colonel Samuel Birch set out to repay the Bedford militia for the shots they fired the week before.[81]

As the retaliatory force bore down on Bedford, they were spotted by American lookouts posted on Guard Hill, but once again the fog of war intervened. Confusing the green jackets of the Loyalists for the green uniforms of the Third American Dragoons, who were en route to Connecticut, the lookouts raised no alarm. Local legend has it that a woman named Esther Holmes caught on and frantically waved her red petticoats to warn the village. Men grabbed their muskets, but their defensive fire was no match for the overwhelming attack. Even without Banastre Tarleton giving directions, the raiders (who included men from the British Legion) made a thorough job of it, burning to the ground every building in the village with the sole exception of a house known to belong to a Loyalist.[82]

Less than a week after the burning of Bedford, one of the most spectacular American victories of the war happened across the Hudson. The narrow channel between Verplanck's Point and Stony Point made it an excellent location for the King's Ferry. Just twelve miles below West Point, King's Ferry

The storming of Stony Point in July 1779 temporarily halted British ambitions in the Hudson Valley. *Library of Congress.*

was a strategically important crossing and, once fortified, served as an outer defense of West Point.

It could also be a springboard for an assault on West Point. The flat fields at Verplanck's Point in particular were a handy place to gather and encamp an attacking force, which could be quickly ferried across to Stony Point for a march up the west bank of the Hudson. With this in mind, in the late spring of 1779, Henry Clinton decided to seize King's Ferry. The Americans had already begun to fortify the place, building Fort Lafayette at Verplanck's Point and beginning construction of a blockhouse at Stony Point, when the British arrived to take both places on June 1.

Washington decided on a response that would make Stony Point untenable for the British. Taking a page from "No Flint" Grey's playbook, he ordered General Anthony Wayne to make a bayonet-only assault to seize Stony Point on the night of July 15–16. Still smarting from Grey's surprise midnight bayonet attack at Paoli two years before, Wayne was happy to repay the British in their own coin.

The meticulously planned maneuver resulted in six hundred British taken prisoner and sixteen pieces of artillery carried off. Not willing to hang around and wait for a British counterattack, Wayne burned the fortifications and abandoned Stony Point two days later.[83]

The British returned and rebuilt their defenses, but the Americans had made their point. One month later, on the night of August 18–19, the Stony Point victory was followed up by Light-Horse Harry Lee's seizure of Paulus Hook, directly across the Hudson from lower Manhattan. Although the operation didn't go as smoothly as Stony Point, it cost the British 50 killed or wounded and 158 taken prisoner, for an American cost of 2 dead and 3 wounded.

The Paulus Hook debacle happened within view of British headquarters across the river and, combined with Stony Point, convinced Clinton that the Hudson Valley was not his path to victory. The Americans were by now too well dug in at West Point, so Clinton turned away from the Hudson and began redeploying troops to pursue a new strategy of conquering the southern colonies. In October 1779, he abandoned both Stony Point and Verplanck.

The British pullback brought no peace to the Neutral Ground. Tarrytown's status as a river port and the entrepot of a wheat growing region, as well as its notably pro-Patriot population, made it an inviting target for British raids intended to punish the rebels while replenishing regimental larders. In November 1779, as part of a wave of expeditions termed the "Grand Forage," a Loyalist raiding party commanded by Major Mansfield Bearmore attacked Tarrytown.[84]

Unfortunately for Bearmore, Armand's Legion was back for a tour of duty in the Neutral Ground. The Throggs Neck–born Bearmore had earned considerable notoriety over the past year, being part of an attack on Young's house the previous Christmas as well as the burning of Bedford in July. Armand's horsemen scattered the Tory raiders and, with the prospect of a high-profile capture, pursued and took prisoner Mansfield Bearmore along with several others. Armand followed up with another strike against Bearmore's troops in their encampment, taking additional prisoners.

Not leaving Armand all the glory, Cornelius Oakley mounted a raid on November 13 against West Farms, hoping to nab James DeLancey in his headquarters in the Archer House,[85] almost beneath the guns of Fort No. 8. Although there was some fierce resistance as Oakley's men stormed the

Archer House, the wily DeLancey had already absconded, and a disappointed Oakley returned north empty-handed.

For both the Queen's Rangers and the British Legion, being an elite unit meant that they were wanted in multiple places. Seeing that the war wasn't going to be won in southern Westchester, Clinton withdrew Simcoe and Tarleton from the Neutral Ground, leaving the field to James DeLancey and his Cow Boys. Clinton now had his eye on a new field of operations. If the Hudson Valley seemed a dead end, the stalemated war could still be won in the Carolinas, where Tarleton's dash and Simcoe's ruthlessness could be valuable assets as the British sought to conquer the southern colonies. Clinton and his expeditionary force set sail from New York the day after Christmas 1779.

For the moment, the British strategic focus was turned away from the Hudson Valley, leaving the Neutral Ground to be fought over by local forces. For James DeLancey, Clinton's departure left him a clear field for action, and with little left to steal in lower Westchester, he would send his Cow Boys in raids against Patriot units.

New Year's Day 1780 dawned on what was the coldest winter of the century, but that hardly cooled the fighting in the Neutral Ground. On January 18, a group of eighty Connecticut troops commanded by Captain Samuel Lockwood attacked a house near Kingsbridge occupied by Loyalists. With the house set ablaze, the Loyalists were forced to surrender, but the Patriot success quickly turned sour when they were pursued by British cavalry, who caught up with them near Mamaroneck, killing twenty-three of the Connecticut men and taking forty prisoners. A disappointed General Heath (back in command in the Hudson Highlands) complained to Washington, "From what I can learn this would have been a very pretty affair, had not folly & imprudence Stain'd the retreat."[86]

The British meanwhile had plans for a pretty affair of their own. Left in command of the British forces while Clinton was campaigning in South Carolina, the Hessian General Wilhelm von Knyphausen took inspiration from his hero, Frederick the Great, and launched his own winter offensive with a series of strikes against American outposts in New Jersey and New York.

Nearly one year to the day after the burning of his West Farms blockhouse, on February 3, 1780, DeLancey's men joined a force of Redcoats and Hessians in a strike against Joseph Young's house at a crossroads that was then known as the Four Corners on Grassland Road (now the site of Blythedale Children's Hospital). Joseph Young had been a prominent militia leader, and his house was a gathering point for American militia forces.

Setting out from Kingsbridge and Morrisania, the expedition against Young's house had to march through knee-deep snow that forced them to leave their fieldpieces behind. At Four Corners, 250 Massachusetts men under Lieutenant Colonel Joseph Thompson were quartered at Young's house and various buildings along Grasslands Road. Surprised by 650 British, they lost 19 dead and 93 prisoners, including Joseph Young himself, who had the added humiliation of seeing his house burned down. A monument on Grasslands Road marks the mass burial of the casualties from both sides. The ruined house would for years remain a local landmark, and the Four Corners became known instead as the Burnt House.

As the year 1780 went on, the back-and-forth raids would take a back seat to a far greater drama that played out in the Neutral Ground, a drama that came close to ending the war in a triumph for King George.

Chapter 7

SPIES

It was hard to say no to George Washington, but Cornelius Oakley did just that. Cornelius had been a valuable member of the Westchester Guides, and Washington, recognizing his bravery and intelligence, suggested that he go incognito behind the lines as a spy. A simple refusal would have sufficed, but Cornelius took the proposal as an insult. He indignantly replied that espionage, as opposed to scouting, was beneath his honor as a gentleman and stormed out of the room. He resigned from the Westchester Guides, although he would reenlist a few months later when his anger cooled.[87]

Modern-day James Bond stories notwithstanding, in the eighteenth century espionage was a despised service. With all its necessary lies, fabrications and betrayals, it was considered a dirty business, unfit for honorable gentlemen. John Jay would later remark that a certain secret agent of his "belonged to a condition in life which rendered him the least reluctant to appear in so equivocal a character. He was poor, ignorant as far as the usual instruction was concerned, but cool, shrewd, and fearless by nature." In short, the agent was no gentleman and thus had no honor to besmirch by being a spy. Regardless of Jay's class disdain, the agent did have a sense of honor. He refused a cash reward for his services, stating that his motives were patriotic, not pecuniary. "It was remarkable," Jay recalled, "that men without moral principles had nevertheless manifested the most disinterested and self-denying zeal in the cause of the country."[88]

In our day, it is difficult to understand how uninformed armies were in the eighteenth century. There were no "eyes in the sky," satellite intelligence, electronic intelligence or any of the plethora of tools modern-day commanders can draw on to surveil and assess the enemy. Information could only be gathered from what individual humans could see, hear or steal, and the intelligence they gathered could travel no faster than a man on horseback.

Espionage was thus an unpleasant but necessary part of war-making, and throughout the war the Neutral Ground of Westchester County would be the haunt of spies and secret agents. At first, though, such activities consisted not of traditional military intelligence but instead were initiated by the civilian government of New York State, which would field one of the war's most famous secret agents.

In 1818, a young gentleman farmer named James Cooper settled down in Scarsdale with the intention of becoming a novelist.[89] His first effort, a Jane Austen pastiche, didn't sell, and friends advised him to leave Regency England alone and seek subjects closer to home that American readers could relate to. As it happened, Cooper was a friend of John Jay, who lived nearby in Katonah. Jay had been a diplomat and Supreme Court judge, but back during the Revolution forty years past he had been a spymaster.

In 1775, John Jay was appointed to head the Committee and First Commission for Detecting Conspiracies. The newly formed government of New York State was keenly aware of the extent of Loyalist sympathies in the lower Hudson Valley, and Jay's committee was tasked with uncovering groups of Loyalists before they could cause trouble for the Patriot cause. To do so, the committee members would have to rely on informers and double agents who could infiltrate Tory firesides and drinking circles.

Years later, Jay would regale James Cooper with stories of those desperate days in Westchester. Cooper, hailing from upstate New York, was a newcomer to the region. Married into a branch of the DeLanceys, a family with its own Loyalist connections, Cooper was eager to learn of the mayhem that went on in the Neutral Ground during what in effect was America's first civil war. The struggle that played out on his own doorstep gave him the idea for a more exciting yarn than any drawing room drama.

Jay's committee would recruit as many as ten agents, but in telling his stories to Cooper, Jay was careful not to name any of them. Fictionalizing the events Jay described, Cooper wove these tales into his novel *The Spy*, considered to be the first bestseller by an American-born author.[90] Almost immediately after the book's publication in 1818, speculation abounded as to the real-life origin of the novel's protagonist, Harvey Birch, an honor eventually claimed by Enoch Crosby.[91]

On his Scarsdale farm, a young James Cooper turned stories of the Neutral Ground into a bestselling novel. *Library of Congress.*

Enoch Crosby was no doubt one of Jay's star agents, but whether or not he had anything to do with the fictional Harvey Birch (both Jay and Cooper vehemently denied this), his entrée into the shadow world of espionage came about by accident.

A veteran of the Canadian campaign, in August 1776 Crosby reenlisted in a unit stationed at Carmel, only to arrive at Carmel to learn that the unit had already moved on to Manhattan to meet the looming British invasion. Heading south on his own, he met up with a man who assumed that Crosby was a fellow Loyalist. Crosby said nothing to dissuade him, and his fellow traveler revealed that he was on his way to join a Loyalist unit forming near White Plains. Sensing an opportunity, Crosby went along with the pretense, only to give him the slip and head back north to the house of Joseph Young at Mount Pleasant. Young was a prominent Patriot, and after Crosby spilled the beans, he guided Young and his posse to bust the Tories in their bivouac. Jay's committee was impressed by Crosby's patriotism and ability to keep a straight face in the presence of the enemy and recruited him as an intelligence operative.[92]

Crosby's prewar profession as a journeyman cordwainer gave him a perfect cover story as an itinerant shoemaker. In rural Westchester, a wandering shoemaker was a welcome visitor, who in return for fixing the family's footwear would gain a shilling or two, a hot dinner and a bed for the night. For Crosby, the main benefit was a chance to listen in on the local gossip and learn who among the "disaffected" were conspiring against the Patriot cause.

On several occasions, Crosby was able to infiltrate Loyalist gatherings and get word out to the Patriot authorities. When the authorities arrived, Crosby was arrested along with the rest, only to engineer an "escape" before the group would go to trial. This could only work a limited number of times before whispered tales of the absconding shoemaker made the rounds and raised doubts. Crosby was accordingly pulled out of the Westchester-Dutchess circuit and reassigned to other areas.

Curiously, in the course of *The Spy*, the fictional Harvey Birch crossed paths with another fictional character who passed into Westchester folklore. In the novel, an interrogation of Birch takes place in an Elmsford taproom dubbed "Flanagan's Hotel," presided over by Betsy Flanagan, who, as local legend would have it, invented the cocktail there in 1779. Cooper's actual inspiration for Betsy Flanagan was likely Catherine Hustler, who during the War of 1812 maintained a tavern in upstate Lewiston. A restaurant named O'Brien's Chateau nevertheless maintained Elmsford's claim to be the birthplace of the cocktail well into the twentieth century, and the legend persists to this day.

Following the 1777 campaign and the British evacuation of Philadelphia, in the summer of 1778 the armies returned to the lower Hudson Valley, and the counterespionage work of Jay's committee was largely subsumed by military intelligence operations run by Washington or his various generals.

Although he didn't serve as part of John Jay's stable of spies, Luther Kinnicutt is sometimes proposed as a model for Harvey Birch. A carpenter hailing from Cortlandt Manor, Kinnicutt enlisted in the Continental forces in October 1778 and at first practiced his trade in his hometown north of Peekskill. Something of a local character around Cortlandt Manor, Luther was known for his cutting wit and personal eccentricities.

Recruited as a spy by General Alexander McDougall, with orders to make "such observations as the good of the service required," Luther used the cover story of a journeyman carpenter for trips through lower Westchester and Manhattan. In New York City, partly destroyed by fire in September 1776, as well as in the rising Loyalist refugee settlement in West Farms, there was plentiful work for a journeyman carpenter—and plentiful gossip to overhear in the taverns. Luther's big coup came in July 1779 when he learned of Banastre Tarleton's impending raid on Pound Ridge. Taking considerable risks to hurriedly make his way from West Farms to Pound Ridge, he arrived two days ahead of Tarleton, but his information wasn't enough to prevent a disaster for the Americans.

However good his cover story and spy craft, a secret agent is always at risk of exposure by another spy, double agent or defector, and unfortunately this proved true for Luther Kinnicutt when in September 1780 his name was among the papers found in John André's boot. Knowing that his name was known to the defecting Benedict Arnold, Kinnicutt's handlers pulled him in from the field just in time to avoid arrest. His ventures into occupied New York were now too dangerous, and Kinnicutt returned to ordinary army duty.

Luther remained a rebel though. After the war, he was arrested for chopping down a toll gate on the Old Croton Turnpike near Croton Falls. He denied the charge, stating that he didn't chop down the gate, as the complaint alleged, but only the post the gate was mounted on. Apart from a modest soldier's pension, Luther never reaped much reward for his services, and he died in the county poorhouse in 1833. Unlike Enoch Crosby, Luther Kinnicutt's grave remained unmarked, and he is believed to be buried somewhere in an old, abandoned cemetery alongside the Saw Mill River.[93]

While Crosby and Kinnicutt acted as outright spies, a more shadowy realm of espionage was that of double agents—men and women who ostensibly were spying for one side while actually serving the other. An American double agent, for example, would defect to the British and volunteer to spy for them. His American handlers would provide him with verifiable bits of information to give the British and establish his reliability. He would then serve as a conduit for false information designed to deceive or confuse the enemy.

Legend has it that George Washington never told a lie, but as the war dragged on, he came to appreciate the value of such disinformation to mislead the British as to his strength or intentions.

Luckily, Washington didn't have to lie too much, as the opposing British commander played right into his hands. Facing a stalemated conflict in the spring of 1779 with reduced numbers of troops, General Henry Clinton was anxious for military intelligence. So much so that he was willing to suspend his natural cynicism when a likely source of information arrived at headquarters. There were plenty to choose from in 1779, due to an increased flow of defectors from the American side, a symptom of declining rebel morale. For the most part, these defectors, seeking to ingratiate themselves with the British, could offer little more than rumor and campfire scuttlebutt, and few if any were properly vetted or debriefed.

To General Alexander McDougall, this represented an intriguing prospect. "The Enemy have had so many Persons of Rank, Trust and Office from us," he remarked to Washington, "that he [Clinton] greedily and credulously embraces, every Intimation of Convertion."[94] It was a golden opportunity to slip a double agent or two into the flow of turncoats, and one such agent would be Elijah Hunter.

A commissioned Continental officer recommended by both McDougall and John Jay, Elijah Hunter was a veteran of the Battle of White Plains and had managed a counterintelligence network protecting the vital Continental supply depot at Fishkill. His bona fides thus seemed impeccable when he was, somewhat reluctantly, recruited by General McDougall to serve as a double agent. Washington hesitated: he distrusted double agents as men of flexible loyalty but recognized their value in spreading disinformation, although it was always possible that the enemy, seeing through their cover stories, could use them to spread *their* disinformation. After personally interviewing Hunter, Washington was still not entirely convinced. He nevertheless gave his assent to Hunter's employment, though advising McDougall to keep such "double spies" on a short leash, as "the less they have it in their power to do us mischief, the better."[95]

Although Washington never fully trusted Hunter, the double agent did deliver some solid information from time to time. His most important revelation was in May 1779, when he alerted Washington of British General Clinton's preparations for a strike up the Hudson to seize the vital river crossing points at King's Ferry (present-day Verplanck) and Stony Point and possibly threaten West Point. The news didn't arrive in time to prevent the seizure of the ferry landings, but Washington was able to shift reinforcements from his camp in New Jersey to secure West Point. It is unclear whether Clinton had the notion of going for West Point in 1779, but the river bottleneck remained an obsession for both sides and the following year it would be the object of the war's most spectacular espionage episode.

The penalty for being caught as a spy was death, as evidenced by a number of execution sites and "hanging trees" that have left their mark on Westchester place names and folklore.

British spies were executed on what is still known as Gallows Hill in Cortlandt Manor. *Photo by the author.*

Gallows Hill in the town of Cortlandt is one such place, and Gallows Hill Road remains on the map today. Originally known as Bald Hill or Drake's Hill, Gallows Hill lay within the American camp that occupied the area between 1777 and 1781. On August 7, 1777, Edmund Palmer, a Westchester native and Loyalist spy, was hanged there. The British royal governor objected to Palmer's execution on the dubious grounds that he held a British officer's commission, but the plainspoken General Israel Putnam minced no words in his reply to Governor Tryon: "Sir: Nathan [*sic*] Palmer, a lieutenant in your service was taken in my camp as a spy: he was tried as a spy; he was condemned as a spy; and you may rest assured, sir, he shall be hanged as a spy. P.S. Afternoon. He is hanged."[96]

A well-known hanging tree was located a few miles from Gallows Hill, on Oak Hill in the town of Peekskill. In January 1777, Daniel Strang, a recruiter for Robert Rogers's Loyalist Queen's Rangers, was hanged from an oak tree on what would later become the site of the Peekskill Military Academy (the school attended by a young L. Frank Baum, who literally followed a yellow brick road there from the train station). A creepy campus landmark, the "Gallows Oak" would outlast the military academy and chill another generation of students when the site became Peekskill High School. The old oak lived on until 2006, when it was finally killed by lightning.

An enormous oak standing on the Purdy homestead in North Salem was put to use to "half-hang" one of DeLancey's raiders. The Nehemiah Loundsbury house on Guard Hill in Bedford was also graced by a large oak tree in the front yard that was utilized by the Americans for summary executions of spies and deserters convicted in courts-martial held in the Loundsbury kitchen.[97]

A renowned "Spy Oak" stood just south of the village of Pelham Manor at what today is Westchester and Buhre Avenues in The Bronx. It was said to have been the scene of more than one summary execution, including a British officer caught out of uniform behind the lines. Documentation of these incidents is lacking, but whoever the executed officer may have been, for years local people pointed to a thick branch, dubbed the "Gallows Limb," overhanging the roadway as the limb on which the alleged spy was hanged. A loop of old telegraph wire was even pointed out as the actual noose. It was said that the hanged lieutenant cursed the tree with his last gasp, and consequently the limb never again sprouted foliage, although the rest of the tree remained healthy until it was cut down as a traffic hazard in 1933.

Over the years, the old tree inspired a number of ghost stories. Some claimed to have been approached by the ghostly figure of a man in British uniform who disappeared into thin air without introducing himself, while others spoke of lamentations heard in the dark of the night. Another legend told of seven Loyalist Cow Boys who were hanged there, one or all of whom would later appear as specters. It was also said to be the execution site of a number of rebel bandits, giving the tree the alternate name of "Skinners Oak."[98]

The Bronx had another legendary hanging tree, again with documentation annoyingly missing. A long-vanished oak tree near the Van Cortlandt House was said to have seen the execution of some thirty Loyalists. An alternative legend placed the hanging tree in present-day Seton Park in Spuyten Duyvil, about a mile from the Van Cortlandt House.[99]

Along with Gallows Hill, Spy Pond and various hanging trees, there are a few Spy Rocks in Westchester where it was said scouts and sentinels of one side or the other eyeballed enemy movements. Major Shelton of the Second Dragoons was supposed to have posted lookouts on Spy Rock in present-day Ward Pound Ridge Reservation to spot Tarleton's oncoming raiders. Another legendary lookout was the Spy Rocks, a prominence between Tripp

Left: The Gallows Oak on the grounds of the Peekskill Military Academy bore its own plaque until it was felled by lightning in 2006. *Courtesy of the Westchester County Historical Society.*

Right: Said to be haunted by the shade of a hanged British spy, the Spy Oak was for many years a local landmark in the eastern Bronx. *Collection of Thomas X. Casey.*

Street and Heather Road in North Castle where American sentinels kept an eye out for approaching British raiders.

For all their best efforts and personal risks, the work of spies did not always produce useful information. Their reports all too often contained inconsequential matters or were too vague or too late to make a difference. Nevertheless, two women serving as spies for King George in the Neutral Ground brought in reports that for varied reasons proved to be consequential indeed.

However vulnerable, women enjoyed certain advantages as spies. The rigid gender roles of the day meant that men assumed that women neither knew nor cared about military matters, making it easy for women to play dumb when accosted by patrols or sentries. Norms of conduct between men and women also made men hesitant to search or closely question a woman, although this could not always be relied on.

One might also spy by proxy. Charity Ferris found herself hostess to the British command in the autumn of 1776 when General Howe made her eastern Bronx home his headquarters. Family tradition had it that she prepared meals for the British officers and had an enslaved servant serve them. She told the servant to keep her ears open and note the conversation among the officers. She would later send the servant out on an ostensible errand during which she would make her way to the American lines and report what she overheard. The name of this involuntary spy has gone unrecorded.[100]

For the British, one of the most successful spy missions of the war would be that of Ann Bates. A schoolteacher in Philadelphia, Ann was married to a man who served as an armorer for the British army. Whatever presumptions might be made as to her military ignorance, thanks to her husband Ann knew her way around an army camp and knew what to look out for.

Ann was inducted into the cloak-and-dagger world while living in British-occupied Philadelphia, assisting the civilian British intelligence operative John Craig. Carrying out some low-level tasks for Craig, Ann impressed her handler with her coolness and devotion to the Loyalist cause.

The shifting tides of the war made Ann a displaced person. When the British pulled out of Philadelphia in the spring of 1778, Ann had to abandon her native town and follow her husband to New York City. Now a homeless Loyalist refugee, Ann volunteered her services as a spy to Major Duncan Drummond, then General Henry Clinton's head of intelligence. Drummond quickly instructed her on what the British were interested in knowing, and the thirty-year-old Ann set forth through the Neutral Ground in the guise of "Mrs. Barnes," a poor widow trying to get by as a roaming peddler.

By that point of the war, there were plenty of such widowed and displaced women making their way along the roads and byways of Westchester County, so Ann aroused little suspicion when she slipped into the American camp above White Plains, selling the soldiers such personal doodads as combs, buttons and needles.

Back in New York City, General Clinton badly needed to know the state of Washington's forces in Westchester. Knowing that a combined French-American attack on Newport, Rhode Island, was imminent, he had just dispatched five thousand troops there to shore up the garrison but worried if in so doing he was leaving New York vulnerable to an attack.

While Clinton dithered, Ann was quietly making her way around the American encampment, doling out needles and shoelaces and taking careful note of regimental flags, pieces of artillery and the general condition of the troops. Little notice was taken of an apparently harmless middle-aged widow, and twice she oh-so-innocently wandered into Washington's headquarters at the Purdy house, once even catching a glimpse of the rebel commander before she was hustled out of the building.

Amid the bustle surrounding Washington's headquarters in White Plains, British spy Ann Bates twice gained entry to the Purdy House, once getting a glimpse of George Washington. *Photo by the author.*

Reporting to British headquarters, Ann delivered to Major Drummond a startlingly detailed assessment of the numbers and equipment of the Americans at White Plains. Reviewing Ann's report, Clinton concluded that Washington was in no position to storm Manhattan Island, ratifying his decision to reinforce the Newport garrison. Those reinforcements ensured a British victory at the subsequent Battle of Rhode Island on August 29, 1778.[101]

Ann made several incursions into Washington's camp that summer, until in September 1778 a British deserter recognized her. As she coolly recalled years later, she was "obliged to make a precipitate retreat for fear of being taken up as a spy."[102]

Not all close-run escapes would be successful; a strange incident late in the war demonstrated the hazards of amateur spy craft, especially for a woman. In August 1781, the Hessian commander Nicholas Dietrich, Baron von Ottendorf (himself a turncoat from the American service), sent a certain "Miss Jenny" to learn what she could of American intentions. The French forces under Rochambeau had recently joined with Washington's army in Westchester, and Miss Jenny, as a native French speaker, seemed an ideal choice to overhear what was being said in the French camp. History knows nothing else about the identity of this Miss Jenny, who was dispatched with the cover story that she and her mother were looking for her long-absent father among the French forces. Jenny's cover story was a thin one and was greeted with disbelief in the French camp. After intense interrogation by both French and American officers, as well as a possible sexual assault, her hair was shorn and she was ridden out of camp in bareheaded shame. Nevertheless, in her report to Ottendorf, she described a camp in readiness for action, and she claimed to have learned from some Hessian prisoners that Washington had personally remarked to them that he would soon be in New York City.

This was an unlikely story, to say the least, and the incident may have been staged for a gullible Miss Jenny as part of Washington's disinformation campaign to fool the British into believing that an attack on New York was imminent. In any event, a credulous Clinton believed it, as it matched what he had been learning from other agents, and he therefore decided not to send reinforcements to Cornwallis, even as Washington was preparing for the march south to Yorktown, Virginia. An unwitting double agent, Jenny's mission was a success, albeit for the wrong side.[103]

Though not actually a spy, Sybil Ludington holds an honored place among intrepid women of the Revolution. As her legend relates, in April 1777, when word came that the British had landed in Connecticut and were marching to destroy the Continental supply depot in Danbury, the sixteen-year-old Sybil volunteered to go on a forty-mile ride to turn out the militia. An unaccompanied forty-mile midnight horseback ride was not the sort of thing young ladies were supposed to do, but Sybil's father, Henry, was the area's colonel of militia and he needed to stay by his home in Fredericksburg (present-day Patterson) to organize the arriving troops.

Alerting the militiamen in their various villages, hamlets and farmsteads, Sybil arrived back home exhausted to the point of tears, and Henry had to help her down from the saddle and carry her safely to bed. Sybil's ride was a partial success; although the militia were too late to prevent the burning of Danbury, they nevertheless intercepted the British as they withdrew and gave them a rough handling at the Battle of Ridgefield, Connecticut, on April 27, 1777, leaving the battered Redcoats glad to get back to their boats on Compo Beach.

Later in the war, Sybil's home in Fredericksburg served as a safe house where the American spy Enoch Crosby would deliver his reports to Colonel Ludington. The house, though, was often under surveillance by Loyalist raiders hoping for a chance to capture the colonel. Sybil and her twelve-year-old sister, Mary, would sometimes stand guard as armed lookouts, and she devised a "code of signals" that would alert Crosby if it were unsafe to approach.[104]

Although the exploits of Ann Bates and Miss Jenny remain unmemorialized, Sybil Ludington is commemorated by a dramatic sculpture by Anna Hyatt Huntington at Lake Gleneida near Carmel, New York, erected in 1961; by a series of New York State historical markers marking her itinerary; and by the annual Sybil Ludington 50K Run, which follows her approximate route.[105]

The twilight world of espionage in the Neutral Ground would culminate in a plot that came close to ending the American dream of independence.

Chapter 8

"WHOM CAN WE TRUST NOW?"

Suddenly, it looked as if the Hudson Valley wasn't such a strategic dead end after all. After Clinton abandoned Stony Point and Verplanck in 1779, it seemed as if he had given up on the Hudson Valley for good. In the autumn of 1780, though, the Hudson would again come into focus when treachery presented a unique opportunity to end the war in a British triumph.

While the Royal Navy had uncontested control over the lower estuary, the Hudson River as it flowed past Westchester offered no smooth sailing. Battling the shifting currents in their dugout canoes, the Native Americans called the Hudson the *Mehicanituk* ("the river that flows both ways") for its strong tidal flows. For vessels sailing upstream, navigation began getting difficult at Croton Point, or Verdrida Hooke ("Vexing Hook" in Dutch), where the narrowing of the river channel made for troublesome currents.

Past Croton Point, if a vessel avoided provoking the Imp of Dunderberg (a legendary entity who could call down a ship-wrecking squall if he felt disrespected) and made it up a reach of the river known as the "Devil's Horse Race," across the Dutchess County line the narrow elbow bend at West Point presented a mariner's nightmare. Navigation around West Point demanded several changes of tack and perhaps a lay-by to await a favorable change of wind. The deep but narrow channel was suggestively named "Martyr's Reach," also known as "World's End." Strong currents added to a three-foot tidal rise presented additional complications to struggling sailors.

Fort Putnam at West Point overlooked the river bend at Martyr's Reach, the keystone of a series of American defenses. *Library of Congress.*

Beginning in 1778, the Americans barred access to Martyr's Reach to vessels coming upstream by an immense iron chain that the soldiers nicknamed "Washington's Watch Chain." The chain itself was something of a marvel of engineering and industrial fabrication, the product of the region's iron furnaces and its deposits of high-quality iron ore.[106]

The chain was guarded by a system of redoubts that overlooked one another on three layers of elevation. Unlike the improvised field fortifications that characterized the early years of the war, the West Point fortifications were professionally designed by a Polish volunteer named Andrew Thaddeus Bonaventure Kosciuszko, who had learned military architecture in Europe, where the art of fortification was reaching its apogee.

Kosciuszko's fortifications ensured that any ship attempting to break the chain would come under punishing fire from multiple redoubts. Together, the fortifications, the chain and the river's curves and currents made the Hudson above West Point as effectively inaccessible to the British as if the Wisconsin Glacier were still blocking the way.

To break the chain and open the river, the hillside forts would first have to be taken. The 1777 battles at Forts Clinton and Montgomery had revealed that the best approach to attacking these forts was from the landward side. To do that, though, the British needed a clear idea of the arrangement of the fortifications. Positioned atop the system of redoubts on the high elevation west of the river, Fort Putnam was the key to the puzzle, and in order to neutralize the downslope defenses, Fort Putman would have to be taken first and quickly. The solution to this conundrum was what Benedict Arnold offered Henry Clinton.

Arnold at this point was a hero of the Revolution and one of the few American generals who made the British nervous. But things had not been going well for Arnold. Hampered by a crippling leg wound he received at the Battle of Saratoga and besmirched by a court-martial instigated by the Pennsylvania civilian government while he was military governor of Philadelphia, Arnold's resentments had been building.

He had also married Margaret "Peggy" Shippen, the daughter of a Loyalist-leaning Quaker family in Philadelphia whose extensive social connections could open a channel of communication to the British command. Among Peggy's connections was Major John André, with whom she had developed a deep friendship during the British occupation. Peggy's best friend was Rebecca Franks, an unapologetic Loyalist whose aunt Phila was married to General Oliver DeLancey. Rebecca, too, had drawn the admiring eye of Major John André and had memorably appeared costumed as a Turkish princess at André's extravagant Meschianza ball in May 1778.

In the wake of the Philadelphia imbroglio, Washington was eager to reassign Arnold to a more prominent role in the army but was surprised when Arnold asked for the command at West Point instead of the field command he had been offered. Arnold had his reasons. With help from his new bride, he had been reaching out to the British with defection in mind. Negotiations had lagged, but command of the strategically crucial West Point meant that he would now have something spectacular to offer, with a price tag to match.

As the plot came to a head, Arnold insisted on dealing in person with Major John André, who was now Henry Clinton's adjutant general in charge of military intelligence. André had at first been dubious about Arnold, but West Point was an opportunity worth taking a few risks for. Nevertheless, for a chief intelligence officer to personally venture behind enemy lines to negotiate with a potential defector would violate both procedure and common sense. Arnold, though, was no ordinary turncoat, and André may have had his own motivations for acceding to Arnold's demands. The capture of West Point (and the tantalizing possibility of seizing George Washington) could be the winning stroke in a stalled war. With victory delivered personally by John André, the king's gratitude could know no bounds—honors, promotion, a knighthood, a rich country estate, maybe even a seat in Parliament. For the humble son of a Huguenot merchant, it was a giddying prospect.[107]

Ferried upstream aboard the sloop-of-war HMS *Vulture*, André landed at a point on the west shore of the Hudson overlooked by Long Cove Mountain, about two miles below the village of Haverstraw. It was a lonesome, little-frequented place, and there André met with Arnold to finalize the arrangements for the betrayal of West Point. Their discussions went on for two hours, partly over disagreements about Arnold's financial remuneration.[108]

With the deal at last finalized, the plan was for André to return to New York aboard the *Vulture* to brief Clinton on the layout of the West Point defenses so he could plan his attack, and at the opportune time Arnold would arrange, through a contrived gap between troop rotations, a brief window of opportunity when Fort Putnam would be unoccupied. With Fort Putnam taken, the west shore defenses could be rolled up like a cheap carpet, while a cavalry raid would intercept Washington's entourage as they returned from meeting with Rochambeau in Hartford. With West Point taken, Washington dead or captured and a British force poised in northern Westchester, the French would likely pack up and go home, and the war would be as good as over.

Carefully laid plans are often undone by unforeseen factors, and a series of unfortunate events would soon unhinge the whole plot. Irked by the sight of the *Vulture* unconcernedly riding at anchor off Teller's Point, the commander of Fort Lafayette on Verplanck's Point sent a pair of cannons down to Teller's Point where, ignoring Arnold's orders not to engage British vessels that night, they opened fire on the *Vulture*. Unwilling to risk his vessel in a pointless duel with a pop-up shore battery, the captain of the *Vulture* raised anchor and had the *Vulture* towed downstream, leaving André stranded in Haverstraw.[109]

Faced with this predicament, André was now about to violate his orders. Having only reluctantly agreed to his meeting with Arnold, Clinton had specifically instructed André that he was not to enter American lines, nor change out of uniform, nor carry incriminating documents. The site of his meeting with Arnold was considered neutral ground, as American sentries patrolled the town of Haverstraw a mile or two to the north.

At that point, André, still in uniform and under a flag of truce, was not in violation of the rules of war. Arnold, though, persuaded André to accompany him to the house of Joshua Hett Smith for a nap and breakfast. The Smith house was within American lines, but even so André could have hidden there until a British ship returned to retrieve him. The timing was tight, though, if the British were to intercept Washington, and in any event, Arnold would not have wanted a uniformed British officer spotted hanging around and prompting awkward questions.[110]

Arnold persuaded André to change into civilian clothes, and with the ferry landing at Stony Point just downhill from the Smith house, he could cross the river and ride down through the Neutral Ground, thus avoiding American forces stationed at Tappan. Arnold was a very persuasive fellow, and even though for the moment he was an enemy officer, as a major general he greatly outranked André and would likely continue to do so once he defected to the British. Arnold was not someone to make an enemy of, and André would not want to risk souring the deal at the last minute. Violating the rest of Clinton's orders, André allowed himself to be persuaded. Bearing passes made out to the merchant "John Anderson" and accompanied by Smith, André set out to the Neutral Ground, with papers detailing the West Point defenses in his boots.

Landing at Verplanck, André and Smith took the road past Peekskill and through the village of Hanover (now Yorktown Heights) to Pine's Bridge crossing the Croton River, pausing for breakfast at the home of Quaker Isaac Underhill. Local legend claims that André was hidden in a secret room of the house of the Loyalist Widow Griffin to await a safe moment to cross Pine's Bridge. The house is long gone, and historians dismiss the unlikely story: André and Smith, in fact, crossed the bridge without hindrance.[111]

The south bank of the Croton marked the beginning of the Neutral Ground, and here a nervous Smith took his leave, advising André to take the road south through White Plains and on down to the British lines at Kingsbridge.

André, however, deviated from the route suggested by Smith. He may have distrusted Smith's advice, knowing from his intelligence work that the slippery Smith worked both sides of the fence, or he may have feared the likelihood of encountering American patrols around White Plains. André instead headed southwest to connect with the less-guarded Albany Post Road at Tarrytown.

André's route through the Neutral Ground would later be marked by plaques and monuments. Heading south from Chappaqua down the Hardscrabble Road, he drew up at the house of Sergeant Sylvanus Brundage of the Westchester militia. Brundage didn't challenge him, and André stopped at a roadside spring to water his horse. The site of "André's Spring" is marked by a small plaque. André continued down to Pleasantville, where he again paused to water his horse (the spot also commemorated with a plaque) before swinging down the Old Bedford Road to Tarrytown.

Ironically, in seeking to avoid trouble, André ran himself into worse trouble. The confusion and ambiguities of the Neutral Ground led to his capture and the undoing of Arnold's plot to betray the Revolution. As an additional irony, the out-of-uniform André was done in by a man likewise out of uniform.

An intemperate remark by Benjamin Tallmadge years later darkened the reputation of André's captors and led many to dismiss them as mere Skinners out for a bit of highway robbery. Nothing could be further from the truth. Acting under orders from Lieutenant Colonel John Jameson to guard the roads between Tarrytown and the Saw Mill River against a reported Loyalist raiding party, Isaac Williams, John Paulding and Isaac Van Wart were Westchester militiamen who, though technically off duty, had volunteered to take part in the patrol. They stationed themselves where the Albany Post Road crossed Clarke's Kill while an additional four militiamen—John Yerkes, James Romer, Isaac See and David Williams—took up a hilltop post where they were joined by the Westchester Guide John Dean.[112]

Benedict Arnold's plot came to grief beneath a Tarrytown tulip tree. *Library of Congress.*

There nevertheless was a profit motive behind their volunteering. New York State had recently decided that militiamen intercepting Cow Boy (or Skinner) raiding parties were entitled to a share of the recovered property (sort of a land-based privateering). Busting Cow Boys bearing loot could result in a nice payday.[113]

Beneath the shade of an ancient tulip tree known by its Native American name of Hokohonkgus, Williams and Van Wart passed the time with a game of cards while Paulding kept an eye on the road. They hadn't been there long when a lone rider appeared, something that in the Neutral Ground was suspicious if not foolhardy.[114]

John Paulding stepped into the road wearing a forest green Hessian Jaeger jacket that he had acquired a few weeks before while making his escape from British custody in Manhattan. With its bright buttons and red facings, it was a flashy garment for an otherwise homespun-clad militiaman and a nifty souvenir of his recent exploit.

The Irish proverb of "whatever you say, say nothing—and *then* say nothing" was a basic principle of espionage work that André blithely ignored. Spotting Paulding's green jacket, André leaped to the conclusion that it signified either a Hessian or a Loyalist and he had therefore encountered a friendly patrol.

Questioned as to which side he was on, André blurted out "the lower party" (Crown forces). Disabused of the idea that he was in friendly hands, André tried to extricate himself but had no effect on the now suspicious militiamen. Displaying his pocket watch (in those days an expensive accessory that only the well-to-do could afford) only convinced the three men that here was something far more important than a passel of marauding Cow Boys. When they searched André, the incriminating papers were quickly pulled out of his boots.[115]

Ignoring André's desperate attempts to bribe his way out of the jam he had gotten himself into, the militiamen took their prisoner to Colonel Jameson two miles away at Sand's Mills in North Castle. Jameson, uncertain as to what the correct protocol would be in this situation, decided to send "John Anderson" to Benedict Arnold with an explanatory letter, while the incriminating papers were forwarded to General Washington.

Jameson's action would have allowed both Arnold and André a chance to escape, but Major Benjamin Tallmadge, arriving at Jameson's headquarters, immediately saw the situation for what it was and persuaded Jameson to recall André back to North Castle. Fearful of offending Arnold should André prove to be innocent, Jameson covered his back by insisting that his letter, minus the prisoner, proceed to Arnold. For the moment, André was lodged in a barn at Thomas Wright's mill (the site is also marked by a plaque mentioning André's captivity).

Benedict Arnold sat down to breakfast at the Beverly Robinson house on the morning of September 25, confident that by now André had successfully made his way to New York. Instead, a courier brought Jameson's letter, and Arnold knew the jig was up. André had been intercepted, and the papers were on their way to Washington, if they were not already in his hands. Keeping a straight face, Arnold rose from the table, and with a quick explanation to his wife, Peggy, rode down to reach his barge at Robinson's Dock, today known as Arnold's Cove. The *Vulture*, which hadn't been there for André, was there for Arnold, and the turncoat general was spirited away to safety in New York City.[116]

"Whom can we trust now?" gasped Washington shortly after he arrived at the Robinson House and had a look at the incriminating papers. Upstairs, Peggy Arnold, left behind with her newborn son, pitched a nervous meltdown (genuine or feigned, historians disagree) and could provide no information. Washington immediately put the West Point defenses on alert, and thanks to the chance encounter in Tarrytown, the British had lost their chance to end the war in one afternoon.

Meanwhile, at South Salem, in the home of Jacob Gilbert (also marked with a plaque), Benjamin Tallmadge at last caught up with "John Anderson" and immediately saw through his thin disguise. Under questioning, André, never a good liar, admitted to his true identity.

The courtly André made a positive impression on nearly everyone he met. He charmed the officers at American headquarters as smoothly as he charmed the Loyalist lasses of Philadelphia. He impressed Benjamin Tallmadge, who readily accepted André's complaint that his Tarrytown captors were a bunch of low-life bandits. Tallmadge, though, had been a classmate of Nathan Hale and calmly told André that as a spy he would meet the same fate as Hale did. Sent to American headquarters at Tappan, André's route to his doom ironically included a stop-over at Fort Putnam (also mentioned on a plaque).

At Tappan, Washington was as immune to André's charms as he was to Peggy Arnold's histrionics. André was lodged in the Mabie house (today the 1776 Tavern) for his court-martial. André's defense that he was acting under a flag of truce held no water for the officers of the court-martial, who condemned him to death, though with a recommendation of mercy. Washington, himself mindful of Nathan Hale, was in no mood to be merciful, and André was hanged at Tappan on October 2, 1780.[117]

The unraveling of Benedict Arnold's treason and the hanging of John André meant that the war did not end in the Hudson Valley in the autumn of 1780. While the focus of the fighting shifted to Virginia and the Carolinas, the violence in the Neutral Ground would continue for nearly three more years.

Chapter 9

PINE'S BRIDGE

Perhaps feeling that his war was slipping away from him, in 1781 James DeLancey planned his boldest operation yet. This was to be no mere cattle raid, but a long-distance strike at some of Washington's best soldiers.

The catalyst was a devastating American raid on Morrisania. Amid the consternation caused by Arnold's treason, there was a renewed focus on the security of West Point, to the detriment of the Neutral Ground. By the end of 1780, the situation in the Neutral Ground had been deteriorating for some time, with DeLancey's Cow Boys roaming and raiding at will. Philip Pell, commissary of prisoners, had a good look at conditions in Westchester in the course of his work arranging prisoner exchanges. Ignoring military chain of command, he addressed an urgent letter directly to New York's Governor George Clinton, saying, "I verily believe that unless something be done, Westchester County, in less than a month, will be totally in the enemy's power."

Something was done. On January 21, 1781, Colonel William Hull, then in command of the American forces along the Croton River, launched a surprise attack on DeLancey's stronghold with a task force of six hundred infantry and cavalry. By the standards of the Neutral Ground, this was a veritable juggernaut, and its mission was to destroy the Cow Boy base of operations and capture James DeLancey.

Moving swiftly down from Pine's Bridge, Hull's men burned thirty-five to forty log huts in the Loyalist encampment, along with DeLancey's rebuilt blockhouse, and seized sixty horses and cattle. A hastily organized Loyalist pursuit ran into an ambush prepared by Colonel Moses Hazen and his "Infernals" and was driven off at a cost of thirty-five killed or captured.[118]

While Hull's raid was a success, James DeLancey, the target of the raid, once again eluded capture. DeLancey had ample reason not to let himself be taken. DeLancey had given his parole after being captured early in 1777 and had promptly violated it. In those days, parole was a courtesy commonly extended to captured officers, and a parolee gave his word as a gentleman not to participate in the war until he was formally exchanged. By resuming his command of the Westchester Refugees, DeLancey made himself liable to execution if captured again, and after years of depredations by his Cow Boys, leniency was unlikely.

Hull's raid was a major humiliation that demanded appropriate retaliation. Another cattle raid would not do —payback for Hull's raid would have to be something truly spectacular. James's cousin Oliver DeLancey Jr. (son of his uncle General Oliver DeLancey) was now Clinton's adjutant general in charge of espionage, and he likely gave James a timely tip that helped him plan his operations.

The happenstance of war gave DeLancey the sort of spectacular target he was looking for. While the Loyalist leader repaired the damage from Hull's raid and plotted his revenge, American troop rotation brought another, more prominent unit to the Pine's Bridge area in place of Hull's brigade.

The First Rhode Island regiment was accounted some of the best soldiers in Washington's service, and it was a historic unit in other ways as well. Facing difficulties in fulfilling its recruitment quota, in 1778 the State of Rhode Island adopted the radical step of recruiting a regiment of African Americans.

The unit would be formed by men of color from both the free and enslaved populations. Slave owners would be given full cash compensation for men joining the regiment, who would be granted their emancipation at the end of their enlistments. Free men of color were also recruited, including Native Americans of the Narragansett Nation. Officers would be of European descent, as would two additional companies absorbed through a merger with another Rhode Island regiment.[119]

There, of course, had been muttered doubts about the discipline and effectiveness of such a regiment, despite the fact that African Americans had been serving in American units from the very outset of the war. Such doubts were put to rest after the First Rhode Island's combat debut in the Battle of Rhode Island on August 29, 1778, in which they counterattacked repeated Hessian assaults and even captured a Hessian regimental flag.[120]

An African American and a Narragansett stand with Colonel Christopher Greene in a monument to the Pines Bridge Massacre. *Photo by the author.*

Distinguished by their valor, the men of the First Rhode Island were also distinguished by their uniforms. The Rhode Island government had fallen short when it came to maintaining the unit, leaving a ragged and ill-equipped regiment to greet the French when they landed at Newport. Seeing past their tatters, General Rochambeau was impressed by the First Rhode Island's discipline and resolve and ordered new uniforms for them. The uniforms were those of the French Marines, in the French field livery of white, topped off with a peaked miter cap bearing the emblem of a large anchor. It made the First Rhode Island truly outstanding.

Its colonel was Christopher Greene, a third cousin of Washington's right-hand man General Nathanael Greene. He came to the job with solid combat credentials—he had led Rhode Island troops to victory against the Hessians in the Battle of Red Bank, New Jersey, on October 33, 1777, and was well respected by his men.[121]

Arriving at Pine's Bridge, Colonel Greene knew he had a problem. On their way in from Connecticut, smallpox had broken out among the First Rhode Island, forcing Greene to quarantine three hundred men, leaving about two hundred with which to guard a twenty-mile stretch of the Croton River on either side of Pine's Bridge. Appraised of the situation by his spies and informants, James DeLancey saw his opportunity.

DeLancey's men had been probing the approaches to Pine's Bridge for some time, and their presence in northern Westchester was no mere bravado. By late 1780, central and southern Westchester had been stripped bare of cattle, forcing the Cow Boys to range into northern Westchester in search of cows and other Patriot valuables. The environs of Pine's Bridge were thus already familiar terrain, and little scouting would be necessary in order to plan an attack.

After an unopposed midnight march from West Farms, DeLancey's chosen men, dubbed with a bit of bombast "the Invincibles," approached Pine's Bridge at dawn on May 14, 1781. Judging the prize great and the risk of capture small, James DeLancey was for once in personal command of his Cow Boys. This would ensure that the plan would be carried out to his specifications, while leaving no doubt at British headquarters as to who deserved credit for the coup.

There was no point in trying to force their way across the narrow Pine's Bridge—previous attempts had come off badly, and the planks would likely have been taken up anyway. Instead, DeLancey stayed behind with a covering force south of the bridge (he wasn't taking *too* many risks) and directed the rest of his men to cross the Croton at Oblenis Ford about a mile west of the bridge.[122]

Fording the Croton River could be a dicey proposition at the best of times, and dicey is what Oblenis Ford proved to be that spring day, with rapid chest-high water that forced some men to remain behind. Fortunately for DeLancey, the ford was unguarded—Greene posted sentries there at night but left it open during the day to economize his reduced forces.

Once on the north bank of the Croton, the well-soaked soldiers split into two groups. One would head upstream to seize Pine's Bridge as a retreat route, while the other proceeded with the attack. Avoiding the main encampment at "Rhode Island Village," the raiders proceeded to Greene's headquarters at the Davenport House, about a mile from the bridge.[123]

Approaching the Davenport House in command of the main party, Lieutenant Gilbert Totten had his own personal revenge in mind. A local man, Totten had come to case the joint a few weeks before, claiming a flag of truce and stating that he was merely on family business. Greene had seen through his flimsy story, but lacking evidence that Totten was a spy, he took him prisoner instead. Totten was quickly exchanged but was offended by what he took to be Greene's ungentlemanly attitude and was even more offended by being put under the guard of African American soldiers.

The exact sequence of events at the Davenport House that morning isn't clear, but gentlemanly warfare had long since departed the Neutral Ground. Taken by surprise, Greene and the men with him fought back as best they could. Felled by multiple sword blows, Greene was thrown over the back of a horse to be taken prisoner, but he soon bled out and was unceremoniously dumped by the side of the road.[124]

At the Widow Griffin's house near the bridge, some thirty Rhode Islanders tried to make a stand but were quickly overwhelmed. Leaving the bodies where they lay, the raiders didn't linger but clattered across the bridge to reunite with DeLancey and make haste for Morrisania, taking with them twenty-three prisoners. To confuse possible pursuit, they swung west and turned south down the Albany Post Road, pausing for a bit of refreshment at the Odell Tavern in Greenburgh.[125]

They left behind ten men dead, including Colonel Greene and his second in command, Major Ebenezer Flagg. The location of their mass burial is uncertain but is believed to be in the vicinity of the Presbyterian Church on Crompond Road, where two memorials honor their sacrifice. In addition, an impressive new statue has recently been placed in downtown Yorktown Heights.[126]

While the attack at Pine's Bridge was indeed a "nasty affair," as historian Allison Albee put it, it did little to cripple the First Rhode Island or alter the situation in the Neutral Ground. After burying their dead, the surviving men of the First Rhode Island would, four months later, play an honored role in the decisive American victory of the war.

The French were on the way. One week after Pine's Bridge, on May 21, Washington met Rochambeau at Wethersfield, Connecticut, to discuss a plan of campaign for the 1781 season. Rochambeau favored a march south to seize Portsmouth, Virginia, in conjunction with the French fleet under Admiral de Grasse. Washington, however, was fixated on taking New York City, and Rochambeau reluctantly deferred to the American commander, agreeing to march his troops from Newport, Rhode Island, to the Hudson. From Dobbs Ferry they would reconnoiter the British defenses of Manhattan and plot a line of attack.

The loss of New York City had been a personal and strategic embarrassment for Washington, and since the fall of 1776, British-occupied Manhattan had tantalized him with the possibility of retaking it and thereby effectively ending the war. Now, with much of the Royal Navy dispersed fighting a

global war and with thousands of European-trained soldiers at his back, it seemed to Washington that the time had come. First, though, a "Grand Reconnaissance" would be needed to probe British defenses and determine a viable route onto Manhattan Island.

The French completed their march in early July, setting up camp in and around Ardsley while the Americans pitched their tents to the west in Dobbs Ferry. To fend off annoyances from British warships, Washington commanded the building of redoubts to oversee the Hudson shoreline. The redoubts were located on the west side of the Albany Post Road, where they could also guard approaches from the south, and were sited at an elevation that would make it difficult for British ships to return fire. A British probe on July 19 resulted in severe damage to the HMS *Savage*, reminding British commanders of the disadvantages of contesting land-based cannons with wooden-hulled sailing ships.[127]

Bringing ten thousand French and American troops down from their Dobbs Ferry encampments, Washington and Rochambeau, together with their staffs, rode through the Neutral Ground and along the Harlem River and Long Island Sound on July 21–23, 1781.

Again the lack of accurate maps would pose a problem, as Robert Erskine's surveys hadn't extended into the Neutral Ground. A local guide was needed, and accordingly, the reconnaissance scooped up the young Westchester Guide Andrew Corsa at his Fordham Manor home. Corsa would direct the two generals as they made a systematic survey of the Manhattan Island defenses.

Also accompanying the expedition was a youthful French captain named Louis-Alexandre Berthier, who served as General Rochambeau's cartographer. Berthier provided information he had gathered while accompanying numerous foraging parties and busily took notes and drew sketch maps as the reconnaissance proceeded. Although little notice was taken of him at the time, twenty years later Berthier would be Napoleon

Opposite: A French force under General Rochambeau came ashore at Newport, Rhode Island, in July 1780, changing the strategic balance of forces. *Library of Congress.*

Above: The route taken by Rochambeau's army is today marked as a National Historic Trail. *Photo by the author.*

Bonaparte's right-hand man, mapping and directing Napoleon's maneuvers across Europe. Present-day American historians acknowledge their debt to Berthier as well—his crisply drawn maps of the 1781 campaign proved crucial in researching the Washington-Rochambeau Historic Trail.[128]

The Grand Reconnaissance brought to Westchester what was perhaps the best-dressed unit ever to prowl the Neutral Ground: Lauzun's Legion, part of Rochambeau's army. Composed of both infantry and cavalry, the foot soldiers were attired in a crisp blue and white livery, while the horsemen were dressed in the eye-catching style of Hungarian hussars. With their gold-embroidered tunics, short jackets (pelisses) worn over the left shoulder and tall shakos, the hussars were dressed to overawe the enemy as they descended with a fast and furious saber charge.

A classic eighteenth-century mercenary force, Lauzun's Legion gathered footloose soldiers of fortune from all corners of Europe, including some fifteen nationalities. Only a third of the troops were French; about half were from various German states and the rest from places as far afield as Ireland, Russia, Denmark and Hungary.

The official language of command in Lauzun's Legion was German, but by unit tradition curses were delivered in Hungarian, which the officers found to be a wondrous resource for lewd and offensive imprecations (*a macska rúgjon meg!*—"may the cat kick you!"—is one of the milder ones). Such curses were often resorted to, as Lauzun's Legion had a reputation for rowdiness.

This colorful array was commanded by Armand Louis de Gontaut, duc de Lauzun. A popular figure in European aristocratic society, Lauzun, like Banastre Tarleton, blew through his inherited fortune before turning to a military career. He distinguished himself in the French capture of Fort St. Louis from the British in Senegal before being promoted to brigadier general and sailing with his newly formed Legion for North America.

Lauzun's second in command was an even more colorful character, Robert Dillon, one of the Irish "Wild Geese" who found service with the French king. Dillon was a noted duelist in a unit whose officers habitually engaged in duels with each other and had nearly missed sailing to America after being wounded in a duel the day before.

Lauzun was tasked with going ahead of the reconnaissance to secure Washington's flank by neutralizing DeLancey's Loyalist force in southern Westchester. Forewarned of what was about to descend on him, or perhaps not wishing to be kicked by the cat, DeLancey evacuated his Morrisania enclave and moved his Cow Boys across the river to the safety of Harlem.

Untroubled by Loyalist opposition, Washington and Rochambeau made their way down the Harlem River shoreline. A crossing at Spuyten Duyvil was deemed too risky and could have left Washington bottled up at the tip of the Manhattan panhandle, a predicament he had only narrowly escaped from in 1776. Fort No. 8, Britain's only remaining bridgehead on the mainland, was too well defended, and to emphasize the point, the British opened up with a stiff cannonade. The pontoon bridge that the fort defended was in any event too easily cut by retreating troops to be depended on.

Moving down to the southern tip of the present-day Bronx, Washington entertained notions of an island-hopping approach to Manhattan, either by way of Montressor's Island or Long Island. The troublesome waters of Hell Gate and the Long Island Sound "Devil's Belt," along with British warships lurking in the harbor, quashed these ideas as well.

If the Grand Reconnaissance didn't reveal a pathway to victory, it at least convinced a nervous Henry Clinton that the allied armies gathered in Westchester were focused on storming New York City. This conviction would prove crucial a few weeks later.

Rochambeau had been doubtful all along about the Manhattan strategy but had been too diplomatic to argue about it. Returning from the inconclusive reconnaissance, a frustrated Washington was now in a mood to consider alternatives. In his diary entry for August 1, he recorded his disappointment. "Therefore," he wrote, "I turned my views more seriously (than I had before done) to an operation to the Southward."[129]

In a humble farmhouse that still stands on Ridge Road in Hartsdale, one of the most important decisions of the war was made shortly after the Grand Reconnaissance. Today known as the Odell House/Rochambeau Headquarters, it was there on August 14, 1781, that Rochambeau received word from Admiral de Grasse that the French fleet would not be sailing north to the New York area but could instead meet the allied army at the Chesapeake.[130]

Conferring with Washington, Rochambeau laid out the possibilities. *If* the French fleet could fend off a British relief force, *if* Henry Clinton could be bamboozled into keeping his forces on Manhattan and *if* the allied forces could make a midsummer march to Virginia in time, they could trap General Cornwallis in Yorktown and force his surrender.

There were a lot of "ifs" in this proposition, and Washington was uncertain of his army's ability to make the arduous march south to Virginia. His idea of storming Manhattan, though, was clearly a nonstarter, and the Yorktown

The Ministers of Apollo lead a commemorative march by the Dobbs Ferry Historical Society marking first mile of the route to Yorktown. *Photo by the author; courtesy of Early American Music and Arts.*

option, however risky, was the best opportunity yet to strike a decisive blow against the British.

The road to victory began in Dobbs Ferry on August 19, 1781. As the troops assembled and marched to the Hudson, many no doubt expected to turn south toward Manhattan, but were instead surprised to be turned north to Verplanck, where they crossed the Hudson and, following the route of the 1776 retreat to the Delaware, continued on to Yorktown.[131]

Washington had mounted an extensive deception campaign to ensure that Henry Clinton remained bamboozled, bracing for an attack on Manhattan even while the Franco-American army slipped past him. By the time Clinton caught on, it would be too late to do anything to save Cornwallis, deprived as he was of British naval support by the French victory at the Second Battle of the Capes on September 5. Cornwallis surrendered his army at Yorktown exactly two months after the French and Americans departed Dobbs Ferry, on October 19, 1781.[132]

It seemed that the war would soon be over, but bloodshed and destruction would continue in the Neutral Ground for another year and a half.

Chapter 10

EVACUATION DAY

The surrender of Cornwallis at Yorktown, Virginia, on October 19, 1781, would mark a final turning point of the Revolution, but it brought no immediate peace to the Neutral Ground. As negotiators sat down in Paris to hammer out a peace treaty, in May 1782 the two armies in New York quietly agreed to suspend major military operations for the time being. There would be no more big battles, but nevertheless a low-intensity conflict would sputter on in the Neutral Ground throughout the closing year of the war.

One of the more interesting personages to serve in the Neutral Ground at this time was an unassuming soldier named Robert Shurtleff,[133] better known today as Deborah Sampson, woman soldier of the Revolution.

Clad in male clothing, in 1782 Deborah slipped away from her home in Middleborough, Massachusetts, and enlisted in the Light Infantry Company of the Fourth Massachusetts. She left no word behind, and the local belief was that she had eloped, which earned her a formal excommunication from the Third Baptist Church of Middleborough.[134]

Deborah was content to let her neighbors believe that she had run off on a romantic escapade, and she would go to extraordinary lengths to preserve the secret of her gender. Posted to the Neutral Ground in the summer of 1782, she was wounded in a skirmish with Loyalists near Tarrytown. Having a sword cut to her head bandaged at a field hospital, Deborah concealed the bullet wound to her leg and dealt with it by herself. Legend has it that she removed the bullet with a penknife and sutured the wound with a sewing needle, although it is likely she surreptitiously borrowed a silver probe at

In the guise of Robert Shurtleff, Deborah Sampson soldiered in the Neutral Ground in support of the American cause. *Library of Congress.*

the hospital.[135] As a result of this do-it-yourself surgery, her leg never fully healed, but her secret was safe for the time being. She was assigned to light duty on the staff of General John Paterson.

One year later she fell ill in Philadelphia, and this time her gender was discovered. Perhaps out of respect to her courage and patriotism, Dr. Barnabas Binney kept her identity confidential until it was time for her to muster out, revealing the truth about "Robert Shurtleff" in a note to General Paterson. Paterson was not amused, but Deborah was nevertheless honorably discharged at West Point on October 25, 1783. Her soldier's pay, ever in arrears, was withheld by Massachusetts on the grounds that as a woman she was not legally enlisted, and it took the intervention of John Hancock to get them to pay up. It likewise took the intervention of her friend Paul Revere to get her granted a military invalid's pension.

Apart from a statue in her hometown of Sharon, Massachusetts, Deborah was honored by having a World War II Liberty ship named for her, albeit in her married name of Deborah Gannett. More recently, she was commemorated in the Deborah Sampson Act of 2021, requiring the Veterans Administration to address issues of gender-based harassment and sexual assault within the agency. Deborah is also brilliantly portrayed in a one-woman play by Judith Kalaora, founder and artistic director of History at Play.

For some in the Neutral Ground, the winding down of the war meant that there was still unfinished business to settle. George Washington had ordered the Westchester Guides to capture or kill James DeLancey, but years of successive attempts brought only frustration as the elusive Cow Boy colonel evaded the net every time.

Obsessed with a mission unfulfilled, on March 4, 1782, Brom Dyckman set out to again try to nail DeLancey. Failing to lure the Tories into an ambush, Dyckman opted on a direct attack on Morrisania. They killed some Cow

Boys and captured about two dozen, but James DeLancey was not among them. Pursued by the enemy, the American raiders rode up the White Plains Road into present-day Mount Vernon, where Brom Dyckman was felled in a sharp skirmish. He died of his wounds in Peekskill on March 9 and was buried at the Yorktown Presbyterian Church nearby the casualties of the Pine's Bridge Massacre.[136]

On October 27, 1782, the Continental army began its final withdrawal from Westchester, completing the transfer on October 28, six years to the day after the Battle of White Plains. The French forces under Rochambeau had departed the week before, heading to Boston and the transports that would take them to new deployments. Retracing the outset of their march to Yorktown the previous year, the now victorious Americans at Dobbs Ferry struck their tents, crossed the Hudson at Verplanck and moved north to what would be their final cantonment at Newburgh.

American raiders would make one last try at apprehending James DeLancey. On January 24, 1783, John Odell, perhaps hoping to avenge the death of his fellow Westchester Guide Brom Dyckman, guided a force of fifty militiamen down from Peekskill in a raid on Morrisania. Again, James DeLancey was not to be found; a story would have it that he escaped the raiders by hiding in a pig pen.[137]

Two months later, on March 23, news arrived of the signing of the peace treaty in Paris. A bitter Henry Clinton departed for England, and a new British commander, General Sir Guy Carleton, arrived to turn the lights out on British-occupied New York. Short of available transport, he quietly began evacuating Loyalists and non-essential military personnel in August. Among the early evacuees would be the Black Loyalists and their families, who would be removed before the Americans arrived to reclaim their human "property." Conferring with Washington, Carleton agreed on a final departure deadline of noon on November 25, 1783.

General Guy Carleton took over command of the British forces in New York and organized the evacuation of Loyalists at the end of the war. *Library of Congress.*

Moving with his troops down from New Windsor, Washington crossed the Hudson and marched through the Neutral Ground. Moving down the Albany Post Road, they passed through scenes of past tragedies and triumphs: Tarrytown, where Benedict Arnold's plot was unhinged in a chance encounter beneath a roadside tulip tree; Dobbs Ferry, from which the march to Yorktown began; Edgar's Lane, scene of the victory over the Hessians; the Philipse mansion in Yonkers, where a young Washington was once a guest of the now-condemned Tory Philipse family; and Kingsbridge, once crossed by a battered American army on its way to a desperate standoff at White Plains.[138]

Ahead of the oncoming Continentals, Carleton evacuated Manhattan in stages, bringing his men down from the northern and middle parts of the island and concentrating them in lower Manhattan for the final departure. Washington followed at a respectful distance, keeping the armies well apart lest an accidental clash ruin the orderly withdrawal. On November 16, Washington joined New York Governor George Clinton to hoist the new nation's flag over a reclaimed Fort Washington. On the morning of November 25, the Continental army followed the route they took to New York in the spring of 1776, proceeding down the Boston Post Road and through the Bowery Gate to New York City.[139]

The New York City that Washington reclaimed bore little resemblance to the flourishing town he had sought to defend seven years before. The intervening years of conflagration, military occupation and overcrowding left a tattered and run-down city, and with the departure of the British troops and Loyalist refugees, a ghostly depopulated town as well.

About sixty thousand Loyalists would immigrate to Britain, Canada or other parts of the remaining empire. Those who remained faced the prospect of prosecution and property confiscation.[140] New York State's constitution mandated death for "treason," but in practice an oath of allegiance would often suffice for a repentant Loyalist to make his peace with the government.[141] Making peace with their Patriot families or communities, though, could be more difficult. In some instances, such at St. Paul's in Eastchester, notorious Loyalists were denied burial in the church grounds, even years after the war. Major John Hungerford fought for King George and immigrated to Nova Scotia. Years later, he quietly returned to his family in Purchase and, as if to spurn the violence he had taken part in, joined the Quakers. By his request, he was buried in an unmarked grave at the Purchase Friends Meeting House Cemetery, near the grave of the Westchester Guide Cornelius Oakley.[142]

Property confiscations were mostly applied to the most egregious cases, such as the Philipse and DeLancey families. Confiscation orders could be legally contested—Alexander Hamilton opposed confiscations as a violation of the Treaty of Paris, and as he established his legal practice in Manhattan,

Above: A victorious George Washington entered liberated New York City on November 25, 1783. *Library of Congress*.

Left: The extensive lands of Frederick Philipse were among the Loyalist properties confiscated at the end of the war. *Photo by the author*.

he would represent wealthy Loyalists fighting confiscations in court. Endangered property could also be sold or leased to a family relation on the American side, as did Robert Edwards, an ancestor of this author, who leased his lower Manhattan real estate to his cousin Colonel Aaron Burr.

Emigrating Loyalists could claim compensation for material losses, but the British government saw to it that the application process was complicated and daunting, with short deadlines that were easy to miss. Out of the sixty thousand Loyalists who left the United States, only about three thousand compensation claims were filed—and not all of these were paid in full, many often not paid at all. For some Loyalists, an alternative was the granting of a temporary annuity. The size of the annuity varied greatly according to the rank and social status of the applicant. General Oliver DeLancey, for example, received a gentleman's income of £500 per year, while others received as little as £20.

Land grants in Canada were another alternative for displaced Loyalists. At North Wallace in Cumberland County, Nova Scotia, there is a monument to more than four hundred Loyalists, mostly from Westchester, who left New York at the beginning of June 1783 on board the ships *Thetis* and *Nicholas and Jane*. After a six-week voyage, they landed at Fort Cumberland on July 15 to receive land grants allotted to them by the British government. The monument inscribes the names of the emigrants, and among them are the names of divided Neutral Ground families, including Purdy, Chatterton, Hatfield, Horton, Angevine, Totten, Ferris and Pugsley.[143]

Another group of refugees from the Neutral Ground obtained a land grant that they named Westchester Valley for their lost homeland. Westchester Valley, along with Westchester Station and Westchester Mountain, remains on the map of Nova Scotia to this day. Loyalist members of the Purdy family were prominent among the settlers, and they are remembered in such place names as the Purdy Family Cemetery in Westchester Station and Purdy Wharf in Halifax.

Beverly Robinson's Loyal American Regiment left New York in the ships *Ann* and *Apollo*, bound for Fredericton, New Brunswick, where they received a land grant known as Block 12. Their colonel, Beverly Robinson, was not among them, having sailed to England. He would never again see his Hudson River home of Beverly House; instead, he settled in modest circumstances near the spa town of Bath.

Long exiled from their sprawling manorial lands in the Neutral Ground, Frederick Philipse III and his family had remained in occupied New York City, hoping for a British victory that would allow them to return home

In Yonkers, *Enslaved Africans' Rain Garden* by sculptor Vinnie Bagwell commemorates the enslaved workers of Philipse Manor, as well as their emancipation following the war. *Photo by the author.*

(and no doubt collect back rent from their tenants). News of the peace treaty meant that that wouldn't happen, leaving Philipse no choice but to abandon the Westchester properties his family had acquired over three generations. Part of the Philipse property seized by New York State was the human "property" of enslaved people, who at the urging of John Jay would be freed in the first state-mandated emancipation in the new nation. Their story is recalled in educational programs at the Philipse Manor Hall State Historic Site in Yonkers and at Philipsburg Manor in Sleepy Hollow and also commemorated by sculptor Vinnie Bagwell's *Enslaved Africans' Rain Garden* in Yonkers.

The Loyalist settlements in Nova Scotia included some three thousand Black people who had enlisted with the British on the promise of emancipation, including a number of people from the Neutral Ground. While the emancipated Black Loyalists were conveyed to Nova Scotia, there were also enslaved persons brought along by their emigrating Loyalist owners. These included four people whom Gabriel Purdy brought to Annapolis Royal on the ship *Caron*. The emancipated Black people found freedom but not equality in Nova Scotia, and by 1790, discrimination and violence prompted one thousand of them to depart for the new free African colony of Sierra Leone.

Notwithstanding the pig pen episode, the news of the peace treaty made it plain to James DeLancey that his Bronx River war was over. Expecting no kindness from the victorious government of New York State, he resigned his colonel's commission on April 3, 1783, and shortly after sailed to London. From England he sailed for Halifax, Nova Scotia, in September 1784 and purchased a 650-acre estate on the Annapolis River, where he died on May 2, 1804. His mansion house there is still standing and can be rented out on Airbnb. His burial place is a signposted grave site at the DeLancey Family Cemetery in Tupperville, Nova Scotia.

He left behind his mother, Elizabeth Colden DeLancey. In her sixties, Elizabeth didn't want to leave her beloved Union Hill, even though the house, repeatedly trashed by Patriot raids, was uninhabitable and she was sheltering with relatives at Coldenham (present-day Montgomery) in Orange County. When the Commissioners of Forfeiture showed up to seize the Bronx River estate, she took them to court on the grounds that she, and not her outlawed son James, was the legal owner of the property.[144]

Elizabeth won her case, only to die the following year, and was buried at St. Peter's Church on Westchester Square. By suing to keep the DeLancey estate intact, she unwittingly performed a public service for the new nation.

The estate was eventually purchased by the Lydig family, and in 1888 it was acquired in whole by New York City as part of Bronx Park, to become the site of the Bronx Zoo shortly after.[145]

The DeLanceys of Mamaroneck remained untainted by the depredations of James and Oliver and remained in their part of the onetime Neutral Ground, where in 1818 Susan Augusta DeLancey would marry James Cooper. Settling in Scarsdale, Cooper would write the bestselling novel that perpetuated the dark memory of the Neutral Ground.

Various individuals would make peace in their own ways. Brom Dyckman's family was, like so many others, divided by the war, and Staats Dyckman broke with his Patriot relatives and served as an accountant for the British army's Quartermaster Department in New York City. The Quartermaster Department was notoriously corrupt, and Staats was no better than the rest of them, keeping two sets of books and pocketing graft on top of his salary. He was canny with his ill-found wealth, however, and surreptitiously helped support his needy rebel relatives. After the war, he talked his way out of a Parliamentary inquiry and was awarded an annuity from His Majesty's government. The Dyckman family remembered Staats's generosity, and in 1788, he was able to return and build Boscobel, a mansion that remains a historic site open to the public in a relocated position near Cold Spring.

Patriot vengeance did not fall equally hard on all Loyalists. Jonathan Fowler owned a large estate in Eastchester that was confiscated in 1780, but Jonathan was not forced to emigrate and he remained on his lands. After the war, New York State allowed him to gift his confiscated estate to his Patriot sons, including the Continental army officer Theodosius, who let Jonathan and his wife live out their lives in peace on a small parcel of the estate.

Stephen Ward's family had also suffered division. Stephen's brother Edmund turned Tory and fled to New York City, leaving his wife, Phebe Fowler Ward, to manage the farm and raise their children without him. Phebe was an avowed Patriot, but nevertheless her farm, legally owned by the Tory Edmund, was confiscated from beneath her feet at the end of the war. Petitioning Governor George Clinton to reverse the confiscation, Phebe could only complain that as Edmund's wife she had no power over his choice of side in the conflict. She was not the only Patriot wife of a Loyalist husband to find herself in such a predicament. Phoebe's brother-in-law Stephen did what he could, seeing to it that part of Edmund's three-hundred-acre estate remained unconfiscated. Stephen in the meantime had the task of rebuilding his house, which had been burned by John Graves Simcoe and his Queen's Rangers.

The casualties of the fighting are honored at commemorative reenactment events throughout the region. *Photo by the author.*

While ill-gotten war profits might build an occasional mansion, throughout the Neutral Ground burned ruins marked the sites of humble farmsteads. Weeds thrived in once productive wheat fields, and grass grew in the roadbed of the formerly well-traveled Boston Post Road. Devastated by years of banditry and civil war, the Neutral Ground would nevertheless regain its prewar population by 1790. Some old colonial families would remain and painstakingly rebuild their lives. Others, attainted as Tories or simply ruined by the war, would leave Westchester to start over again on the expanding frontier or in Loyalist-friendly Canada, their places taken by new incomers drawn to the fertile fields of the lower Hudson Valley.

In time, Westchester would gain a reputation as a prosperous producer of fruit, vegetables and dairy. The railroads brought the rise of comfortable suburban homes and posh estates, while places such as Yonkers, Mount Vernon, West Farms and Morrisania became thriving industrial communities. The bad old days of the Neutral Ground would be largely forgotten.

But it would never be entirely forgotten. Memory of the Neutral Ground would be perpetuated in history books and stirring novels, and its fought-over places would be memorialized by plaques, monuments, historical markers, place names and historic buildings, as well as by local folklore and legend. Today, a plethora of historical societies, "friends of" organizations and reenactment units strive to preserve the historical buildings, artifacts and memory of the American Revolution in The Bronx and Westchester County.

Today, amid the 250th anniversary of the American Revolution, we pause to honor the graves of Patriots and remember that the Revolution was won less by declarations, proclamations and dramatic events but through the bitter civil conflict endured by ordinary people in such places as the Neutral Ground.

Appendix

WHO WAS THE HEADLESS HORSEMAN?

One of the most enduring and beloved legacies of the Revolutionary War in Westchester is the legend of the Headless Horseman, first written up by Washington Irving as "The Legend of Sleepy Hollow" in his 1820 *The Sketch Book of Geoffrey Crayon, Gent.*

A Hessian decapitated in a "nameless battle," the Horseman is said to be condemned to forever ride the midnight roads and byways of the Neutral Ground in search of his severed head. (Anyone who has misplaced their eyeglasses will appreciate the difficulties involved in such a quest.)

The Horseman's origins are conjectural. The Battle of White Plains is considered a likely beginning, where a Hessian artilleryman was in fact decapitated by an American cannonball in the closing action of the battle on the day after Hallowe'en, November 1, 1776. The incident, interestingly enough, happened conveniently near the original road leading to Tarrytown, on the map today as Old Tarrytown Road. An alternative theory places his fatal mishap at the Battle of Edgar's Lane, an easy ride down the Albany Post Road from Sleepy Hollow.

The Headless Horseman of Sleepy Hollow, though, is far from unique, and his true origins may lie as far afield as Ireland, Scotland or England.

In Ireland, the tale was told of the Dullahan, an ancient Celtic deity that demanded sacrifices by decapitation. Displaced by St. Patrick, the evil Dullahan was condemned to ride about on horseback carrying his own severed head. The apparition of the Dullahan was said to be a portent of disaster.

A marker at Sleepy Hollow Cemetery recalls the enduring legend of the Headless Horseman. *Photo by the author.*

On the west coast of Scotland, the Isle of Mull is haunted by Ewen of the Little Head (*Eoghan a'Chinn Bhig* in Gaelic), who lost his head in a clan battle in 1538 and who rides the trackways of Mull in search of his severed noggin. Unlike the Dullahan, sightings of Ewen are considered a good thing, or at least good for a round of drinks in the pub.

In England, the southwestern county of Devon boasts not one but two Headless Horsemen. One haunts the spooky moorlands of Dartmoor, and the other is said to be a priest beheaded in the Middle Ages for some unnamed offense, who quietly travels an old road near the town of Torquay. For good measure, there's a headless coachman too, who haunts the vicinity driving a one-horse carriage.

Dutch and German settlers in New Amsterdam may have brought with them the tale of *Der Kopfloser Reiter* (the headless rider), who looms up out of the woods to warn travelers of danger.[146]

Hessians are popular subjects of Revolutionary War ghost stories, and tales of a headless Hessian have also been told in Basking Ridge, New Jersey, where folks claim that their headless horseman was the inspiration for Irving's story. Beheaded in a skirmish, the Hessian's body was carried by his horse into the Great Swamp, where it said that his headless apparition appears in an area known as the Devil's Den.

Newark, Delaware, also has its own headless horseman, although in this instance it was an American named Charlie Miller, beheaded by a cannonball in the battle of Cooch's Bridge on September 3, 1777. It is said that poor headless Charlie may be seen along the I-95 median strip in Newark and along wooded sections of the old Welsh Tract Road. A beheaded British dragoon is also believed to haunt Wedgefield Plantation in South Carolina.

Washington Irving often drew his inspirations from local sources, and a ghoulish prank in New York City may also be the Horseman's point of origin. On January 2, 1800, the body of a young woman named Gulielma Sands was found in a well in Manhattan's Lispenard Meadows. The case caused a sensation, especially after the accused killer, Levi Weeks, was acquitted. It's remembered as New York City's oldest cold case, and the well and its environs were soon alleged to be haunted; people tended to avoid the spot, all the more so when a local joker pulled his cape collar up over his ears and took to galloping past the well to scare people as a headless horseman. Near the site, the young Washington Irving frequented the Bull's Head Tavern, soaking up many a tall tale told over mugs of muddy ale, and doubtless he would have heard the story of the headless prankster of the Manhattan Murder Well.

Today, the image of the Headless Horseman embellishes the street signs of Sleepy Hollow, and a "headless" rider sometimes makes an appearance at the village's annual Old Dutch Church Days in October, along with dramatic recitations of Irving's tale by local historian/storyteller Jonathan Kruk at Irving's home of Sunnyside in Irvington. The Headless Horseman is also commemorated by an eighteen-foot steel sculpture by local artist Linda Perlmutter on Route 9 just below the Old Dutch Church and by a granite bas-relief by Michael Gressel at the entrance to Philipsburg Manor. He moreover enjoys the rare distinction of being commemorated by two historical markers, one at one of two reputed Headless Horseman bridges and another inside the Old Dutch Church Burial Ground.

NOTES

Chapter 1

1. Today's Westchester Square in the Bronx.
2. Samuel Seabury stayed on after the war and became the first bishop of the reorganized Episcopal Church based at Trinity Church on Wall Street. His great-great-great-grandson Samuel Seabury, nicknamed "the Bishop" for his righteous demeanor, would in the 1930s be the investigative judge who pulled down Jimmy Walker.
3. Often misread as "governor," Gouverneur Morris's name was probably pronounced "gover-NEER."
4. Brookhiser, *Gentleman Revolutionary*, 23.
5. Raftery, *Cemeteries of The Bronx*, 107.
6. Diaz, "Can You on Such Principles," 12.
7. Raftery, *Cemeteries of The Bronx*, 177.
8. Legend has it that one visitor was a young Scottish merchant named John Loudon McAdam, who was said to have built the very first "macadamized" road on the estate's driveway as a present to his prospective father-in-law. McAdam's bride, Anna Charlotte DeLancey, however, was the niece, not the daughter, of Peter DeLancey, and she wasn't born until 1786 in England. Perhaps coincidentally, though, the street that was later built over the eastern end of the driveway would be named Adams Street.
9. The site of Union Hill is within the present-day Wild Asia section of the Bronx Zoo.
10. McNamara, *McNamara's Old Bronx*, 9.
11. It took western movies and the novels of Zane Grey to change the meaning of cowboy, and curiously, an early silent film star who was instrumental in this change, William S. Hart, spent his later childhood on the Bronx River in West Farms, at the very spot where DeLancey's Cow Boys once set forth. While recalling his days on the Bronx River with fondness, Hart's memoirs give no indication that he was aware of this historical connection.

12. Diamant, "Skinners," 50–61.
13. Albee, *Nasty Affair*, 8.
14. Today, it is known as the Thain Family Forest in the New York Botanical Garden. The Bears' Den is at the northern end of the Spicebush Trail.
15. Huguenin, "Cowboys of the Ramapos."

Chapter 2

16. Hufeland, *Westchester County During the American Revolution*, 186.
17. Crotty, "Times of Peril," 10–11, 45–71.
18. Leaves from the Ferris Family Tree, "Grove Farm Home to Many a Ferris," http://www.ferrisfamily.us/grove-farm-home-to-many-a-ferris.
19. Raftery, *Cemeteries of The Bronx*, 3:108.
20. Mount Vernon *Daily Argus*, September 4, 1951.
21. Ultan, "Perils of the Revolution."
22. Hagist, "Outbreak!"
23. Elliott, "Lessons from an Outbreak."
24. Passing through several hands after the war, Beverly House burned down in 1892. A plaque and a historical marker now mark the site by Route 9D.
25. Clyne, *Caves for Kids in Historic New York.*
26. Hulda's story first appeared in print in Edgar Mayhew Bacon's 1897 book *Chronicles of Tarrytown and Sleepy Hollow*. Although Bacon made no claim that it was genuine history, he noted no source for the story, although he might have picked it up from local oral folklore.
27. Jansen, "Hulda the Witch."
28. Although there is no trace of her cabin in what is now termed "Hulda's Glen," hikers can follow the Witch's Spring Trail in Rockefeller State Park to get to Spook Rock.

Chapter 3

29. The Negro Fort was so called because it was manned by a company of formerly enslaved Virginians who had enlisted with the British army. A small redoubt sited alongside the original Boston Post Road, it served as a "speed bump" protecting Fort No. 4.
30. The site of the redoubt is marked by a monument in the Heliotrope section of Woodlawn Cemetery. It is sometimes said to be the inspiration for the place name of Gun Hill, but the name preceded the Revolution. The Valentine House remains today as the Valentine-Varian House Museum of Bronx History.
31. Hufeland, *Westchester County During the American Revolution*, 192.
32. Smith, "Major Robert Rogers."
33. A lost relic of the Revolution was the so-called Revolution House, which stood directly opposite Williams Bridge on the east side of the Bronx River. Painted red, it was said to be scarred with bullet holes from the 1777 firefight.

The Revolution House was demolished in the early 1900s to make way for the extension of Gun Hill Road east of Williams Bridge.

34. Some accounts, including the memorial plaque erected in his honor, have Captain Crawford killed in a later skirmish at the Ward House on November 18, 1777. Westchester historian Otto Hufeland places his mortal wounding at the March incident, and the present-day Friends of the Ward House agree with the March date. Hufeland, *Westchester County During the American Revolution*, 198.
35. The exact numbers killed at the Ward House are uncertain but may be as high as forty to fifty, with twenty-seven captured. In 1908, a reported fifty burials were unearthed in what was termed "the Soldiers' Burying Ground" near the junction of the White Plains Post Road and Main Street in Tuckahoe. The remains were eventually turned over to the Bronx Chapter of the Daughters of the American Revolution, which had them reinterred at St. Paul's Church in Mount Vernon. In 1922, an additional three Revolutionary War burials were found at Midland Place, including the bones of a young boy. They were supposed to have been reburied in an unmarked spot by the Tuckahoe War Memorial, but a few years later it was alleged that the bones had been lost and were never in fact reburied. Raftery, *Cemeteries of The Bronx*, 1:8.
36. Sheehan, "American Perspective on the Peekskill Raid."
37. In 2019, two skeletons believed to be casualties of the Battle of Ridgefield were found beneath a home on Main Street. Following forensic study, the remains are expected to be reinterred for the 250th anniversary of the battle in 2027. Kaitlyn Lyle, *Ridgefield Press*, August 8, 2023.
38. Marx, "Too Little, Too Late."
39. Smith and Johnson, "Interpreting the Battle for the Hudson River Valley."
40. Hufeland, *Westchester County During the American Revolution*, 204.

Chapter 4

41. British surveyors produced the superb *British Headquarters Map* in 1782 depicting Manhattan Island and adjoining areas of Long Island and the mainland, but not interior Westchester.
42. Reportedly, a set of tunnels bearing Revolutionary War artifacts was found beneath the site of the Oakley Tavern when the Carylon Hotel was built in the early 1800s. Traces of what may have been these tunnels were rediscovered when the foundations were dug for the Bonwit Teller building in the 1940s. Crandell, *This Is Westchester*.
43. McKernan, "Oakley Family." John Cromwell, a cousin of Oliver Cromwell, also emigrated and settled in the present-day Bronx.
44. McDonald and Seymour, *MacDonald Papers*, 1:68.
45. Browne, "Role of Westchester Guides," 27.
46. Weiselberg, "Revolutionary Westchester."
47. The Dyckman family returned to their northern Manhattan farm after the war, and their 1785 house is now the Dyckman Farmhouse Museum.

48. Raymond, *Souvenir of the Revolutionary Soldiers' Monument*, 65.
49. Lucas Buresch, Archive Sleuth, June 1, 2011, https://archivesleuth.wordpress.com/2011/06/01/john-dean-rock.
50. McDonald and Seymour, *MacDonald Papers*, vol. 2, ch. 7, 75.

Chapter 5

51. James Thatcher's Military Journal, June 12, 1778, https://www.americanrevolution.org/james-thatchers-journal-1778/#june. Putnam's Rock apparently vanished in the building of the Hudson River Railroad in 1849.
52. Fryer and Dracott, *John Graves Simcoe*, 38.
53. Edward St. Germain, "Muskets, Rifles, Pistols & More," American Revolution Weapons, www.americanrevolution.org/weapons/#rifles.
54. Though often referred to as "Bloody Ban," the nickname first saw print in the 1950s, and there is no evidence of it being used during the Revolution. Knight, "Banastre Tarleton."
55. In eighteenth-century military parlance, a legion was a self-contained combined arms unit incorporating cavalry, infantry and field artillery, the precursor of the modern division.
56. Two of Tarleton's Loyalist officers were the brothers Charles and James Macdonald. They were the sons of Flora Macdonald, famed for shepherding the fugitive Bonnie Prince Charlie to safety following the collapse of the 1745 Jacobite Rising in Scotland. Flora and her husband subsequently immigrated to North Carolina, where, as Loyalists, they found themselves again on the losing side of an uprising. Fraser, *Flora Macdonald*, 175.
57. Sometimes spelled "Emmerick."
58. *Pennsylvania Ledger*, October 29, 1777.
59. Never again commanding his own unit, Emmerich eventually returned to Europe, where he wrote a book, *The Partisan in War; or the Use of a Corps of Light Troops to an Army* (London, 1789). Back home in Westphalia, Emmerich turned rebel and came to a bad end in 1809 when he tried to raise a revolt against the occupying French. Part of his plot was the attempted kidnapping of Napoleon's brother Jerome Bonaparte, who had been installed on the throne of Westphalia. The plot failed, and Emmerich was shot by a firing squad.
60. After the war, Armand made his peace with the king and returned to Brittany, where he formed the Breton Association to oppose the centralizing tendencies of the French revolutionary government. In January 1793, he died of a heart attack allegedly brought on by news of the execution of King Louis.
61. Rindfleisch, "Stockbridge-Mohican Community."
62. In 2021, Daniel Ninham was honored by an impressive statue in Fishkill. Prior to that, he was honored by the name of Ninham Mountain in Putnam County, where a commemorative ceremony took place for many years at an annual powwow. The battle is also commemorated by a monument on Van Cortlandt Park East. The names of the dead of what is referred to as the

"Bronx Massacre" are inscribed on the Mohican Veteran's Memorial of the Stockbridge-Munsee Community Band of Mohican Indians in Wisconsin, where the remaining Wappingers relocated after the war. Back in The Bronx, people have claimed to have heard midnight war cries resounding from the now-wooded battle site in Van Cortlandt Park.

63. The burial site is believed to be not at the present-day monument but rather in a marshy area about a quarter-mile northwest of it. Raftery, *Cemeteries of The Bronx*, 96.
64. Nathaniel Gist was the son of the frontiersman Christopher Gist, who guided the young George Washington during the French and Indian War. Nathaniel was later rumored to be the father of Sequoyah, who created the Cherokee syllabary.
65. The location of the incident was on the ominous-sounding Overkill Road, named innocently enough for a bridge crossing a nearby stream. The road acquired a more gruesome connotation following the massacre and was later changed to the more family-friendly Rivervale Road. In 1972, suburban development turned up the remains of six of Baylor's men, who were respectfully reinterred and memorialized at what today is Baylor Massacre Park.
66. McCoy, "Impact of Logistics on the British Defeat," 25.
67. Though not related to General Charles Lee, he was related to Richard Henry Lee, president of the Continental Congress, and was the father of Robert E. Lee.
68. An alternative, if unlikely, version of the Headless Horseman legend has it that the Horseman was decapitated by a sword blow at Edgar's Lane. Rhinevault and Rhinevault, *Hidden History of the Lower Hudson Valley*.
69. The battle site would not be known as Edgar's Lane until years later, when the farm lane was named in honor of local landowner William Edgar. In addition to a DAR plaque and a NYS historical marker, the Battle of Edgar's Lane has recently been commemorated by the installment of six interpretive panels authored by the historian Erik Weiselberg. Titled "Revolutionary Walk," the panels are located at the intersection of Broadway and Warburton Avenue in Hastings-on-Hudson. I am especially indebted to the Revolutionary Hastings Committee of the Hastings Historical Society and the excellent battle maps drawn by cartographer Robert Romagnoli.
70. St. Clair's military career would end in ignominy a few years after the Revolution, having commanded at the Battle of the Wabash, also known as the "Columbia Massacre," or the "Battle of a Thousand Slain." A punitive expedition against Native Americans in Ohio, the battle would be the worst defeat of an American army by Native Americans.
71. *Royal Gazette* (New York), December 30, 1778.

Chapter 6

72. Lefkowitz, *Colonel Hamilton and Colonel Burr*, 146.
73. DeLancey would get a sort of revenge a year later when in February 1780 British raiders burned Young's house. Lederer, *Place Names of Westchester County*, 161.

74. Burr's round of activities possibly included courting visits to his future wife, Theodosia Prevost, at her home in present-day Ho-Ho-Kus, New Jersey, no easy commute even today with the benefits of bridge and automobile.
75. Isaac's younger brother Abraham "Brom" Martling is said to be the inspiration for "Brom Bones" in Washington Irving's "The Legend of Sleepy Hollow."
76. Canning and Buxton, *History of the Tarrytowns.*
77. McDonald and Seymour, *MacDonald Papers*, 38.
78. McDonald and Seymour, *MacDonald Papers*, 42.
79. Tarleton kept the flag and carried it home after the war. It remained on display at the Tarleton homestead, Breakspears, until 2006, when Tarleton descendant Christopher Tarleton Fagan had it auctioned for a reported $12.36 million to an anonymous bidder.
80. Shonnard and Spooner, *History of Westchester County*, 476.
81. Evelyne H. Ryan, "The Burning of Bedford Village History Re-examined," *Record Review*, July 9, 2004.
82. Hinitt and Duncombe, *Burning of Bedford.*
83. Anthony Wayne earned his nickname of "Mad Anthony" at Stony Point, leading his men despite a seriously bleeding head wound.
84. The name is believed to be derived from the Dutch word for wheat, *tarwe.*
85. Named for John Archer, the founder of Fordham Manor, the Archer House stood at present-day Burnside and University Avenues.
86. Braisted, "Relation of Disagreeable Circumstances."

Chapter 7

87. Rösch, *Historic White Plains*, 100.
88. Beard, *Letters and Journals of James Fenimore Cooper*, 1:44.
89. Cooper's Angevin Farm was located about where the Fenway Golf Club is today. Originally named the Fenimore Golf Club, a recent proposal to change the name back to Fenimore was voted down, but Cooper's residence is locally commemorated by Leatherstocking Lane and Mohican Trail. Cooper did not adopt the middle name of Fenimore until 1826. Carlson, *Conscience of America*, 9.
90. Susanna Rowson's *Charlotte Temple* (1791) preceded *The Spy* as a bestseller, but Rowson was born in England.
91. Crosby's ghost-written memoir, *The Spy Unmasked*, came out in 1828 and established his claim to be the model for Harvey Birch, but not everyone was convinced and there have been other claimants. Crosby's exploits were real enough, though, and he is commemorated by historical markers in both Southeast and Carmel; his grave site at Carmel's Gilead Cemetery is annually honored by the Enoch Crosby Chapter of the Daughters of the American Revolution. There is also Harvey Birch Hill located, appropriately enough, at the intersection of Harvey and Crosby Roads in North Salem. *The Spy* itself is commemorated by a monument outside the Scarsdale Public Library.
92. Barnum, *Spy Unmasked*, 208–17.

93. Raftery, *Cemeteries of Westchester County*, 2:4; Harris, *God's Country*, 37.
94. "To George Washington from Major General Alexander McDougall, 21 March 1779," in Chase and Ferraro, *Papers of George Washington*, 557–60.
95. "From George Washington to Major General Alexander McDougall, 25 March 1779," in Chase and Ferraro, *Papers of George Washington*, 608–09.
96. Hufeland, *Westchester County During the American Revolution*, 217–18. As a spy, Palmer had the rare distinction of being buried with a grave marker, although the stone would be separated from the now lost grave site and resides today in the Peekskill Museum. Spy Pond atop Gallow Hill further commemorates this incident.
97. Raftery, *Cemeteries of Westchester County*, 1:32.
98. Twomey, *Bronx in Bits and Pieces*, 213; Bell, *Haunted History of Pelham*, 36.
99. Kingsbridge Historical Society, "Hangings in Van Cortlandt," https://kingsbridgehistoricalsociety.org/forums.
100. Raftery, *Cemeteries of The Bronx*, 55.
101. Two hundred years later, Ann's report would be of decisive value to the White Plains Historical Society by documenting Washington's residence at the Purdy House in 1778, confirming its claim to the title of "Washington's Headquarters."
102. McBurney, "Ann Bates."
103. "Ottendorf-Miss Jenny Deposition," William L. Clements Library, https://clements.umich.edu/exhibit/spy-letters-of-the-american-revolution/gallery-of-letters/ottendorf-miss-jenny-deposition.
104. Collins, *Enoch Crosby*, 163. Exactly what these signals consisted of has gone unrecorded.
105. Dacquino, *Patriot Hero of the Hudson Valley*. As with many Revolutionary War stories, documentation of Sybil's ride is thin, and some historians have raised doubts as to whether it took place at all or whether she actually visited the sites marked with historical markers by New York State in the 1930s. In 1996, the national Daughters of the American Revolution declined a request by the Enoch Crosby DAR chapter in Carmel Lake, New York, to mark Sybil's grave as that of a National Patriot, citing insufficient evidence of her ride. This was in spite of the fact that Sybil and her ride had been commemorated by a medal in the series "Great Women of the American Revolution" sponsored by the DAR and issued by the Franklin Mint in 1974. Nevertheless, a copy of Anna Huntington's statue is on display in the Washington, D.C., headquarters of the National Society of the Children of the American Revolution. Curiously, neither Sybil's Revolutionary War widow's pension application nor its associated documents make any mention of her ride.

Chapter 8

106. The West Point chain was the second chain to be stretched across the river following the failure of the chain between Fort Montgomery and Anthony's Nose,

which was broken by the British in the 1777 battle. Authentic links of the West Point chain may be seen today at Trophy Point overlooking Martyr's Reach on the grounds of the U.S. Military Academy.

107. André's rank of major was only a temporary "brevet" rank to enable him to serve as Clinton's adjutant. If the war ended at that point, André's rank would revert to his regular rank of captain, with a captain's half-pay pension.

108. The large boulder where André and Arnold conferred is known as Traitor's Rock and is inscribed by an unknown hand, "André, the spy landed here, Sept. 21, 1780." A Rockland County historical marker alongside the Hudson River Greenway Trail also marks the pathway to the "Treason Site."

109. A popular though disputed account, along with a monument at Teller's Point, credits John Jacob "Rifle Jack" Peterson, a militiaman of African and Kitchawan Native American descent, and his buddy George Sherwood with raising the alarm and obtaining the cannons. At Sparta Cemetery in Scarborough, the tombstone of Abraham Ladew has a hole in it, said to have been caused by a cannonball fired from the *Vulture*, though not likely from this particular incident.

110. Demolished in 1929, the site of the Smith residence, or "Treason House" as it was locally known, is now the campus of the Helen Hayes Rehabilitation Hospital.

111. Albee, *Nasty Affair*, 59.

112. The exact spot is about two hundred yards east of the present-day monument on Broadway. Canning and Buxton, *History of the Tarrytowns*, 39.

113. DiSanto, "Major André's Captors Revealed."

114. Kruk, *Legends and Lore of Sleepy Hollow*, 38. Hokohonkgus stood for many years as a revered "witness tree" known as "André's Tree" until it died from a lightning strike in 1905. The spot is still shaded by a large tulip tree, planted as a replacement for Hokohonkgus.

115. The Captors' Monument on the border of Tarrytown and Sleepy Hollow was erected in 1853 on land donated by the Taylors, a free Black family. The statue depicting John Paulding was added in 1880, with an inscription that it was donated by John Anderson. This namesake of André's *nom de guerre* was a wealthy New York tobacco merchant who in the 1840s employed in his shop Mary Rogers, "the beautiful seegar girl" whose unsolved 1841 murder inspired Edgar Allan Poe to write "The Mystery of Marie Rogêt." Dogged by rumors of his involvement in the case, Anderson eventually barricaded himself in his Tarrytown mansion against what he thought was the accusing ghost of Mary Rogers. His Greek Revival mausoleum in the Green-Wood Cemetery has an unusual double portico, as if to provide a backdoor escape in case the vengeful spirit of Mary Rogers followed him to Brooklyn.

116. Arnold's flight may be traced on the Glenclyffe Loop Trail, accessible from the Arden Point trail at the Garrison Metro North Station. A brochure detailing a self-guided history hike is available from the Putnam History Museum (www.putnamhistorymuseum.org).

117. André was originally buried beneath the gallows, but years after the war, his body was recovered and entombed in an elaborate monument in Westminster Abbey. A black granite memorial marks the site of his hanging and initial burial site, an unusual and perhaps unique monument to an enemy spy. For years, it was believed that a toe bone was left behind when André's remains were transferred. Encased in a tiny sarcophagus, it was treasured as a local family heirloom, but it turned out to be a piece of wood. Gerard, "True Story of Major André's Toe Bone," 3.

Chapter 9

118. Hazen's Infernals was the nickname of a regiment of pro-American Canadians.
119. A reenactment unit of the First Rhode Island is active today, located in Trenton, New Jersey.
120. An impressive monument to the First Rhode Island stands on the battlefield in Middletown, Rhode Island, nearby what is still called Bloody Brook.
121. In June 2022, the remains of thirteen Hessian casualties of the battle were turned up in what is now Red Bank Battlefield Park.
122. The site of Pines Bridge and its associated fords today lie beneath the Croton Reservoir. The modern bridge that carries Route 100 across the reservoir approximates the location of Pines Bridge.
123. The Davenport House still stands as a private residence, not open to the public. The route to the Davenport House ran through a rocky defile that became known as Spook Rocks, said to be haunted by the ghosts of the men who died that day. Albee, *Nasty Affair*, 106.
124. Virgintino, "Revolutionary War Massacre at Pines Bridge."
125. Albee, *Nasty Affair*, 108. The building still stands today at Broadway and Clinton Avenue.
126. Albee, *Nasty Affair*, 97.
127. Borkow, *George Washington's Westchester Gamble*, 134. A monument marking the site of these redoubts may be seen today at the junction of Broadway and Livingstone Avenue in Dobbs Ferry.
128. Borkow, *George Washington's Westchester Gamble*, 130.
129. Borkow, *George Washington's Westchester Gamble*, 139.
130. Borkow, *George Washington's Westchester Gamble*, 136. The Friends of the Odell House/Rochambeau Headquarters is working to restore the house and open it as a museum. Washington's headquarters was in the nearby Appleby house, which has since been lost to time. A radio station currently occupies the site. An 1895 monument outside the Hyatt-Livingston House on Broadway was erected in the mistaken belief that it was the site of Washington's headquarters; the house burned down in 1974, and the plaque was revised in 2000 to remove the reference to Washington's headquarters and instead memorialize the Franco-American encampment.

131. The first mile of the march is annually commemorated by the Dobbs Ferry Historical Society's "Road to Freedom" event.
132. A longtime Bronx legend has it that decoy American campfires twinkled from Vault Hill in today's Van Cortlandt Park to fool British observers in the Van Cortlandt House.

Chapter 10

133. Spellings vary.
134. Moody, *Massachusetts' Deborah Sampson*, 16.
135. Moody, *Massachusetts' Deborah Sampson*, 19.
136. Hufeland, *Westchester County During the American Revolution*, 429.
137. Hufeland, *Westchester County During the American Revolution*, 432.
138. Baker, *Itinerary of General Washington*, 311. Uncertainty surrounds a long-cherished Bronx belief that Washington slept at the Van Cortlandt House on his way to reclaim New York City in 1783. The house, in today's Van Cortlandt Park, is maintained as a museum by the National Society of Colonial Dames in the State of New York, where what an earlier generation might recall as "Washington's Bedroom" is now simply termed "the West Chamber."
139. Evacuation Day was a civic holiday in New York City until the 1920s, when it gradually petered out and was forgotten in favor of Thanksgiving (and Thanksgiving shopping). In recent years, there have been initiatives to revive it. An official Evacuation Day reception is held at city hall every November 25. In 2008, the Brigade of the American Revolution held a commemorative reenactment in lower Manhattan for the 225th anniversary. In 2009, the Fraunces Tavern Museum began an annual walking tour that follows Washington's route from city hall to the Battery. In 2019, the Lower Manhattan Historical Association revived the annual celebration with a parade through lower Manhattan.
140. Flick, *Loyalism in New York*.
141. Jouet, "Revolutionary Criminal Punishments," 13–20.
142. Raftery, *Cemeteries of Westchester County*, 2:56.
143. McConnell, "Cairn to Westchester Loyalists in North Wallace."
144. A miniature portrait of her, painted on ivory the year before her death, is in the collection of the Metropolitan Museum of Art.
145. The DeLancey family lands in lower Manhattan were seized and sold, although the memory of the family is preserved in the names of Delancey (*sic*), James and Oliver Streets, and additionally in a mural depicting the DeLancey estate in the Delancey Street subway station.

Appendix

146. Alexander, "Six Terrifying Tales of Headless Horsemen."

BIBLIOGRAPHY

Books and Publications

Albee, Allison. *The Nasty Affair at Pines Bridge*. Yorktown Historical Society, 2005.

Atkinson, Rick. *The British Are Coming: The War for America, Lexington to Princeton, 1775–1777*. Henry Holt and Company, 2019.

Baird, Charles Washington. *History of Rye, Westchester County, New York*. Anson D.F. Randolph & Company, 1871.

Baker, William Spohn, ed. *Itinerary of General Washington from June 15, 1775, to December 23, 1783*. J.B. Lippincott, 1892.

Barnum, H.L. *The Spy Unmasked*. Harbor Hill Books, 1975.

Beard, James Franklin, ed. *The Letters and Journals of James Fenimore Cooper*. Vol. 1. Belknap Press of Harvard University Press, 1960.

Bell, Blake. *The Haunted History of Pelham, New York*. State University Press of New York, 2022.

Borkow, Richard. *George Washington's Westchester Gamble*. The History Press, 2011.

Brookhiser, Richard. *Gentleman Revolutionary: Gouverneur Morris—the Rake Who Wrote the Constitution*. Free Press, 2003.

Browne, George W. "The Role of Westchester Guides During the American Revolution." Master's thesis, University of Rhode Island, 1962.

Canning, Jeff, and Wally Buxton. *History of the Tarrytowns: Westchester County from Ancient Times to the Present*. Harbor Hill Books, 1975.

Carlson, Rod. *The Conscience of America: How James Fenimore Cooper Became Our Founding Novelist*. Rod Carlson, 2016.

Chase, Philander D., and William M. Ferraro, eds. *The Papers of George Washington*. Revolutionary War Series. Vol. 19, *15 January–7 April 1779*. University of Virginia Press, 2009.

Clyne, Patricia Edwards. *Caves for Kids in Historic New York*. Library Research Associates, 1980.

Collins, Paul E. *Enoch Crosby the Shoemaker Spy*. Page Publishing, 2020.
Crandell, Richard F. *This Is Westchester: A Study in Suburban Living*. Sterling Publishing, 1954.
Dacquino, Vincent T. *Patriot Hero of the Hudson Valley: The Life and Ride of Sybil Ludington*. The History Press, 2019.
Ewald, Johann. *Diary of the American War: A Hessian Journal*. Edited by Joseph P. Tustin. Yale University Press, 1979.
Ferling, John. *Almost a Miracle: The American Victory in the War of Independence*. Oxford University Press, 2007.
Flick, Alexander Clarence. *Loyalism in New York During the American Revolution*. Columbia University Press, 1901.
Fraser, Flora. *Flora Macdonald: "Pretty Young Rebel": Her Life and Story*. Alfred A. Knopf, 2023.
Fryer, Mary Beacock, and Christopher Dracott. *John Graves Simcoe, 1752–1806: A Biography*. Dundurn Press, 1998.
Gara, Donald J. *The Queen's American Rangers*. Westholme Publishing, 2015.
Harris, Jay. *God's Country: A History of Pound Ridge, New York*. Pequot Press, 1971.
Hatfield, Abraham. *The Hatfields of Westchester*. New York Genealogical and Biographical Society, 1935.
Hinitt, Dorothy Humphries, and Frances Duncombe. *The Burning of Bedford, July 1779, as Reported in Contemporary Documents and Eyewitness Accounts: A Salute to the Bicentennial, 1976*. Bedford Historical Society, 1974.
Hufeland, Otto. *Westchester County During the American Revolution, 1775–1783*. Westchester County Historical Society, 1926.
Knight, John. *War at Saber Point: Banastre Tarleton and the British Legion*. Westholme Publishing, 2020.
Kruk, Jonathan. *Legends and Lore of Sleepy Hollow and the Hudson Valley*. The History Press, 2011.
———. *Legends and Lore of the Hudson Highlands*. The History Press, 2018.
Kwasny, Mark V. *Washington's Partisan War, 1775–1783*. Kent State University Press, 1996.
Lederer, Richard M. *The Place Names of Westchester County*. Harbor Hill Books, 1978.
Lefkowitz, Arthur S. *Colonel Hamilton and Colonel Burr: The Revolutionary War Lives of Alexander Hamilton and Aaron Burr*. Stackpole Books, 2020.
Martin, Joseph Plumb. *A Narrative of Some of the Adventures, Dangers and Sufferings of a Revolutionary Soldier*. Glazier, Masters and Company, 1830.
McDonald, John MacLean, and William Seymour, eds. *The McDonald Papers*. White Plains, Westchester County Historical Society, 1926–27.
McNamara, John. *McNamara's Old Bronx*. Bronx County Historical Society, 1989.
Moody, Pauline. *Massachusetts' Deborah Sampson*. Privately published, 1975.
O'Shaughnessy, Andrew Jackson. *The Men Who Lost America: British Leadership, the American Revolution, and the Fate of the Empire*. Yale University Press, 2013.
Raftery, Patrick. *The Cemeteries of The Bronx*. Westchester County Historical Society, 2016.

———. *The Cemeteries of Westchester County*. Westchester County Historical Society, 2011.

Raymond, Marcus D. *Souvenir of the Revolutionary Soldiers' Monument Dedication at Tarrytown, New York, October 19, 1894*. 1894.

Rhinevault, Carney, and Tatiana Rhinevault. *Hidden History of the Lower Hudson Valley: Stories from the Albany Post Road*. The History Press, 2012.

Rösch, John. *Historic White Plains*. Harbor Hill Books, 1939.

Rose, Alexander. *Washington's Spies: The Story of America's First Spy Ring*. Bantam Dell, 2006.

Scharf, J. Thomas. *History of Westchester County, New York*. L.E. Preston and Company, 1886.

Schecter, Barnet. *The Battle for New York: The City at the Heart of the American Revolution*. Walker & Company, 2002.

Shonnard, Frederic, and Walter Whipple Spooner. *History of Westchester County, New York from Its Earliest Settlement to the Year 1900*. New York History Company, 1900.

Spring, Matthew H. *With Zeal and With Bayonets Only: The British Army on Campaign in North America, 1775–1783*. University of Oklahoma Press, 2008.

Twomey, Bill. *The Bronx in Bits and Pieces*. Rooftop Publishing, 2007.

Ultan, Lloyd. *The Northern Borough: A History of the Bronx*. Bronx County Historical Society, 2005.

Articles

Alexander, Jane. "Six Terrifying Tales of Headless Horsemen." *Atlas Obscura*, September 1, 2023.

Braisted, Todd W. "A Relation of Disagreeable Circumstances: The Attack on Young's House, February 3, 1780." *Journal of the American Revolution* (March 27, 2018).

Crotty, Joseph John, IV. "'Times of Peril': Quakers in British-Occupied New York During the American Revolution, 1775–1783." *Quaker History* 106, no. 2 (Fall 2017).

Diamant, Lincoln. "Skinners: Patriot 'Friends' or Loyalist Foes?" *Hudson Valley Regional Review* 4, no. 2 (September 1987).

Diaz, Michael. "'Can You on Such Principles Think of Quitting a Country?': Family, Faith, Law, Property, and Loyalists of the Hudson Valley During the Revolution." *Hudson River Valley Review* 28, no. 1 (Autumn 2011).

DiSanto, Victor J. "Major André's Captors Revisited: Separating Myths from Historical Reality." *Journal of the American Revolution* (July 12, 2022).

———. "The Rise and Fall of John André's Captors in Popular Culture." *Journal of the American Revolution* (September 6, 2022).

Elliott, Steven. "Lessons from an Outbreak: Smallpox in the Hudson Highlands, 1781." *Journal of the American Revolution* (July 1, 2020).

Geary, Pastor Jeff. "The Gilbert Hatfield House Part II: Mistakes and Legacy." *Pastor Jeff's Blog*, July 6, 2017. https://revgeary.wordpress.com.

———. "The Gilbert Hatfield House: An Obituary." *Pastor Jeff's Blog*, July 4, 2017. https://revgeary.wordpress.com.

Gerard, Alice. "The True Story of Major André's Toe Bone." *South of the Mountains* 65, no. 1 (January–March 2021).

Hagist, Don N. "Outbreak! New York 1779." *Journal of the American Revolution* (April 22, 2020).

Huguenin, Charles A. "The Cowboys of the Ramapos." *Pace* 20, no. 3 (Summer 1969).

Jansen, Tiffany R. "Hulda the Witch: A Look at the Legend Buried in Sleepy Hollow." *Westchester Magazine* (October 22, 2021).

Jouet, Mugambi. "Revolutionary Criminal Punishments: Treason, Mercy, and the American Revolution." *American Journal of Legal History* (June 2021).

Knight, John. "Banastre Tarleton: Top Ten Myths." *Journal of the American Revolution* (August 18, 2016).

Longstreth, Bevis. "Thomas Machin and His Chains." *Journal of the American Revolution* (November 20, 2020).

Marx, Stephen Paul. "Too Little, Too Late: the Battle of the Hudson Highlands." *Journal of the American Revolution* (November 30, 2013).

McBride, Grietje R. (Purdy) and Robert C. McBride. "A Family Divided by the American Revolution: Sergeant Gabriel Purdy UE of the Guides and Pioneers and Colonel James DeLancey's Regiment." *Loyalist Gazette* (Spring 2007): 25–31.

McBurney, Christian M. "Ann Bates: British Spy Extraordinaire." *Journal of the American Revolution* (December 1, 2014).

McConnell, Brian. "Cairn to Westchester Loyalists in North Wallace, N.S." United Empire Loyalists' Association of Canada. https://www.uelac.org/PDF/Cairn-to-Westchester-Loyalists-in-North-Wallace-NS.pdf.

McCoy, Major Eric A. "The Impact of Logistics on the British Defeat in the Revolutionary War." *Army Sustainment* (September–October 2012).

McKernan, Maureen. "The Acker Family." *Mount Vernon Daily Argus*, August 28, 1951.

———. "The Oakley Family." *Peekskill Evening Star*, July 31, 1951.

———. "The Odell Family." *Peekskill Evening Star*, August 14, 1951.

———. "The Purdy Family." *Peekskill Evening Star*, August 7, 1951.

———. "The Van Wart Family." *Mount Vernon Daily Argus*, September 4, 1951.

Melvin, Tessa. "A Truce Is Called in Historical Battle." *New York Times*, November 2, 1986.

Poirer, Noel B. "A Legacy of Integration: The African American Citizen-Soldier and the Continental Army." *Army History* (Fall 2002).

Rindfleisch, Bryan. "The Stockbridge-Mohican Community, 1775–1783." *Journal of the American Revolution* (February 3, 2016).

Sheehan, Michael J.F. "An American Perspective on the Peekskill Raid." *Journal of the American Revolution* (May 13, 2015).

Smith, Gregory, and James M. Johnson. "Interpreting the Battle for the Hudson River Valley: The Battle of Fort Montgomery." *Hudson River Valley Review* 20, no. 1 (2003).

Smith, Scott M. "Major Robert Rogers and the American Revolution." *Journal of the American Revolution* (November 23, 2021).

"A Spy Wins a Purple Heart: The Amazing Tale of Daniel Bissell and the Military Order of Merit." *Journal of the American Revolution* (June 2, 2015).

Tomback, Sharon. "Miller House in the American Revolution." *North Castle History* 37 (2010). North Castle Historical Society.

Ultan, Lloyd. "Perils of the Revolution." *Bronx Press-Review*, July 8, 2008.

Virgintino, Mike. "Revolutionary War Massacre at Pines Bridge." Classic New York History. https://classicnewyorkhistory.com.

Weiselberg, Erik. "Revolutionary Westchester: John Odell, General Washington's Westchester Guide." *Hudson Independent*, May 15, 2020.

INDEX

A

Albee, Allison 101
André, John 30, 45, 79, 90, 91, 92, 93, 94, 95, 96
André's Spring 92
Archer House 45, 72, 73
Armand's Legion 55, 72
Arnold, Benedict 30, 79, 90, 91, 92, 93, 94, 95, 96, 97, 110
Associated Loyalists 22

B

Babcock's Hill 58
Bates, Ann 84, 85, 86, 87
Baylor Massacre 59, 61
Bearmore, Mansfield 63, 72
Bear Mountain 38, 40
Bears' Den 24
Bedford 34, 69, 70, 72, 82
Berthier, Louis-Alexandre 102
Birch, Harvey 76, 77, 78
Birch, Samuel 70
Bishop, Sarah 30, 31
Bolton, Reginald Pelham 64
Boscobel 115
Bowery Gate 110
British Legion 50, 52, 53, 69, 70, 73
Bronx River Gorge 20, 24
Brundage, Sylvanus 92
Burnt House 74
Burr, Aaron 65, 66, 112

C

Caledonian Legion 53
Calver, William Louis 64
Campbell, Archibald 36
Canvass Town 28
Carleton, Guy 109
Christian, Marcus 29
Clapp's Tavern Road 55
Coldenham 114
Committee and First Commission for Detecting Conspiracies 76
Constitution Island 38
Continental Light Dragoons 54
Continental Village 40
Cooper, James 24, 76, 77, 78, 115

Corsa, Andrew 46, 102
Cow Boys 23, 24, 25, 29, 63, 65, 66, 73, 82, 94, 97, 98, 100, 104, 108, 109
Crawford, John 69
Crawford, Samuel 36
Crosby, Enoch 76, 77, 78, 79, 87
Croton Point 88

D

Davenport House 100, 101
Dean, John 45, 93
Dean, William 45
DeLancey, Alice 20
DeLancey, Elizabeth Colden 21, 114
DeLancey, James 18, 97, 109, 114
DeLancey, Oliver 90, 112
DeLancey, Oliver, Jr. 98
DeLancey, Peter 20, 21
DeLancey's Brigade 22
DeLancey's Refugees 22, 23, 58
DeLancey, Susan Augusta 115
DeLancey, Warren 20
Devil's Belt 105
Devil's Horse Race 88
Dietrich, Nicholas, Baron von Ottendorf 86
Dillon, Robert 104
Dobbs Ferry 60, 101, 102, 109, 110
Drummond, Duncan 84, 85
Dyckman, Abraham "Brom" 28, 43, 44, 45, 64, 108, 109, 115
Dyckman Farmhouse Museum 64
Dyckman, Michael 43, 45
Dyckman, Staats 115

E

Edgar's Lane 44, 60, 110
Edwards, Robert 112
Emmerich, Andreas 50, 51, 53, 54, 56, 58, 60
Emmerich's Chasseurs 50, 53, 56
Enslaved Africans Rain Garden 113, 114
Erskine, Robert 42, 102
Ewald, Johann 61

F

Ferris, Charity 83
First Rhode Island 98, 99, 101
Fishkill 40, 43, 80
Flagg, Ebenezer 101
Flanagan, Betsy 78
Flanagan's Hotel 78
Fort Clinton 40
Fort Hill 38
Fort Independence 34
Fort Lafayette 71
Fort Montgomery 38
Fort No. 4 34
Fort No. 8 36, 45, 65, 72, 105
Fort Putnam 90, 91, 95
Fort Washington 17, 110
Four Corners 73, 74
Fowler, Jonathan 115
Fowler, Theodosius 115
Fowler, Thomas 29
Franks, Rebecca 90

G

Gallows Hill 81, 82
Gallows Oak 82
Gilbert, Jacob 95
Gist, Nathaniel 58
Grand Forage 72
Grand Reconnaissance 46, 102, 104, 105
Greene, Christopher 99, 100, 101
Grey, Charles 59, 71
Guard Hill 70, 82
Guides and Pioneers 48

H

Hadden, Elijah 70

Hamilton, Alexander 18, 110
Hatfield Tavern 43
Haverstraw 91
Hazen, Moses 98
Heath, William 33, 34, 43, 45, 73
HMS *Savage* 102
Hokohonkgus 94
Holmes, Elisha 70
Holmes, Esther 70
Honourable Board of Associated Loyalists 23
Horse Neck 67
Hudson River Chain 89
Hulda of Bohemia 31, 32
Hull, William 97, 98
Hungerford, John 110
Hunter, Elijah 80
Hunt, Marianna "Myanna" 28

I

Imp of Dunderberg 88
Indian Field 58

J

Jameson, John 93, 94, 95
Jay, John 75, 76, 77, 78, 80, 114
John Dean Rock 46

K

King's Ferry 70, 80
Kinnicutt, Luther 68, 78, 79
Knyphausen, Wilhelm von 73
Kosciuszko, Andréw 89

L

Lady Washington's Dragoons 58
Lauzun's Legion 104
Lee, Charles 52, 62, 63
Lee, Henry "Light-Horse Harry" 60, 61, 72
Lispenard Meadows 28, 121
Lockwood, Ebenezer 68, 69
Lockwood, Samuel 73
Long Cove Mountain 91
Loyal American Regiment 30, 112
Ludington, Sybil 38, 86

M

Mabie house 95
Martelaer's Rock 38
Martin, Joseph Plumb 50
Martling, Isaac 68
Martyr's Reach 88, 89
McDougall, Alexander 34, 37, 78, 80
Mertz, Balthasar 60, 61
Miller, Ann Fisher 62, 63
Miss Jenny 86, 87
Montressor's Island 105
Morris, Gouverneur 19, 20
Morris, Lewis 19, 20
Morris, Sarah Gouverneur 20
Morris, Staats Long 20

N

Ninham, Daniel 55, 58
Nova Scotia 110, 112, 114

O

Oak Hill 81
Oakley, Cornelius 42, 72, 75, 110
Oakley, Isaac 42
Oakley Tavern 42
Oblenis Ford 100
Odell, Isaac "Uck" 44, 60
Odell, John 43, 44, 45, 58, 109
Odell Tavern 101

P

Palmer, Edmund 81
Paulding, John 93, 94

Paulus Hook 24, 60, 72
Peekskill 36, 38, 40, 78, 81, 92, 109
Peekskill Landing 37
Peekskill Military Academy 81
Philipsburg Manor 114, 121
Philipse, Frederick, III 112
Philipse Manor Hall 63, 114
Pine's Bridge 92, 97, 98, 99, 100, 101
Popolopen Creek 38
Post, Peter 60, 61
Pound Ridge 68, 69, 70, 79
Pugsley, James 27
Purdy, Abagail 50
Purdy, Gabriel 114
Putnam, Israel 67, 81
Putnam, Rufus 42, 50
Putnam's Rock 50
Pyle's Massacre 60

Q

Quakers 18, 26, 27, 43, 90, 92, 110
Queen's Rangers 29, 34, 35, 36, 50, 51, 52, 55, 56, 73, 81

R

Rebel Hollow 24
Rhode Island Village 100
Ritzema, Rudolphus 53
Robinson, Beverly 30, 40, 50, 95, 112
Rochambeau, Compte de 46, 86, 91, 99, 101, 102, 104, 105, 109
Rocking Stone 20
Rogers, Robert 29, 34, 35, 81
Romer, James 93
Royal American Reformers 53

S

Sampson, Deborah 107, 108
scabies 30
Schuldam 41
Seabury, Reverend Samuel 18
See, Isaac 93
Sheldon, Elisha 54, 68
Sheldon's Horse 54
Shippen, Margaret "Peggy" 90
Simcoe, John Graves 50, 51, 52, 53, 54, 55, 56, 58, 60, 65, 73
Skinner, Cortlandt 24, 94
Skinners 23, 24, 25, 28, 63, 93
Skinners Oak 82
smallpox 29, 99
Smith, Claudius 24, 25
Smith, Joshua Hett 91, 92
Spuyten Duyvil 17, 33, 54, 82, 105
Spy Oak 82
Spy Pond 82
Spy Rock 82
Spy, The 24, 76, 78
St. Clair, Arthur 63
Stockbridge Indian Company 55
Stony Point 40, 68, 70, 71, 72, 80, 88, 92
Strang, Daniel 81
Sugar Loaf Mountain 30, 50

T

Tallmadge, Benjamin 68, 93, 94, 95
Tarleton, Banastre 50, 51, 52, 53, 54, 56, 58, 60, 62, 65, 68, 69, 70, 73, 79, 82, 104
Thatcher, James 49
Thompson, Joseph 74
Totten, Gilbert 100
Tryon, William 40, 66, 81
Tuffin, Charles Armand 55
typhoid 29
typhus 29

U

Underhill, Isaac 92
Underhill, Nathaniel 68
Union Hill 21, 114

V

Van Cortlandt House 82
Van Wart, Isaac 93, 94
Verdrida Hooke 88
Verplanck's Point 40, 68, 70, 71
Vulture 91, 95

W

Ward, Edmund 115
Ward House 36
Ward, Phebe Fowler 115
Ward, Stephen 26
Washington-Rochambeau Historic Trail 104
Wayne, Anthony 59, 71, 72
Westchester Chasseurs 22
Westchester Refugees 22, 50, 98
Westchester Valley 112
West Point 30, 38, 40, 70, 71, 72, 80, 88, 89, 90, 91, 92, 95, 97, 108
Whaleboat War 41
Widow Griffin's house 92, 101
Williams Bridge 36
Williams, Daniel 63
Williams, David 93
Williams, Isaac 93
World's End 88

Y

Yerkes, John 93
Young, Joseph 63, 65, 72, 73, 74, 77

ABOUT THE AUTHOR

Stephen Paul DeVillo is a local historian, author of *The Bronx River in History and Folklore* (The History Press), *The Battle of White Plains: Washington and Howe in Westchester* (The History Press) and *The Bowery: The Strange History of New York's Oldest Street* (Skyhorse Publishing). He is a longtime walking tour guide for the Bronx River Rambles and has given numerous talks and webinars on topics of Revolutionary War and local history. As a firm believer in on-the-ground research, his particular interest is the Revolutionary War and its events in the New York area.